Origins of SelFLESHness

Origins of SelFLESHness

Based upon the Scriptures

Written by:
Derek Lawrence-Harper
The Minister Artist

DERECK LAWRENCE HARPER

Dedication

This book is dedicated to men and women whose spirit is conflicting with their flesh. The flesh is selfish and therefore the term "selFLESHness" was created. People who are willing to face their struggle with sin, addictions, perversion, and pornography will learn the origins of human struggle through scriptures and doctrines.

Preface

This book is dedicated to men and women whose spirit is conflicting with their flesh. The flesh is selfish and therefore the term *selFLESHness was* created. People who are willing to face their struggle with sin, addictions, perversion, and pornography will learn the origins of human struggle through scriptures and doctrines. Satan has used sexual sins as a tool to steal, kill, and destroy God's children.

Please be advised this book is targeted for people who need healing and those who can handle the meat of the God's word to minister to those in need. Also be advised that some of the artwork is explicit and suggestive but contain a biblical reference. Furthermore, this book references Biblical scriptures, Apocryphal scripture, new hypotheses, personal

experience of the author, and address some mythological creatures that may or may not be real.

This book will provide head knowledge to the individuals that read it but I have learned that head knowledge will not save you. I encourage everyone who reads this book to also research on their own. My ministry is READ it 4 YOURSELF which is a church without walls to encourage people to read, pray, and serve your fellow man the way that Christ did while he walked this earth. I want people to stop living in guilt and seek the Lord while he can still be found. His grace is sufficient for us all and He has already paid the price for our sins and all we have to do is accept Him as out Lord and Savior. Therefore, I warn you again that this is not traditional teaching.

Some of the information presented in this book may be difficult to accept. Henceforth, I suggest that you pray to The Father through His Son and ask for the

confirmation of the Holy Ghost. If you do not get an immediate answer put it on the shelf and wait for an answer. My hope is this book will be a blessing to you.

Table of Contents

Chapter One: Introductory Overview of Our Battle

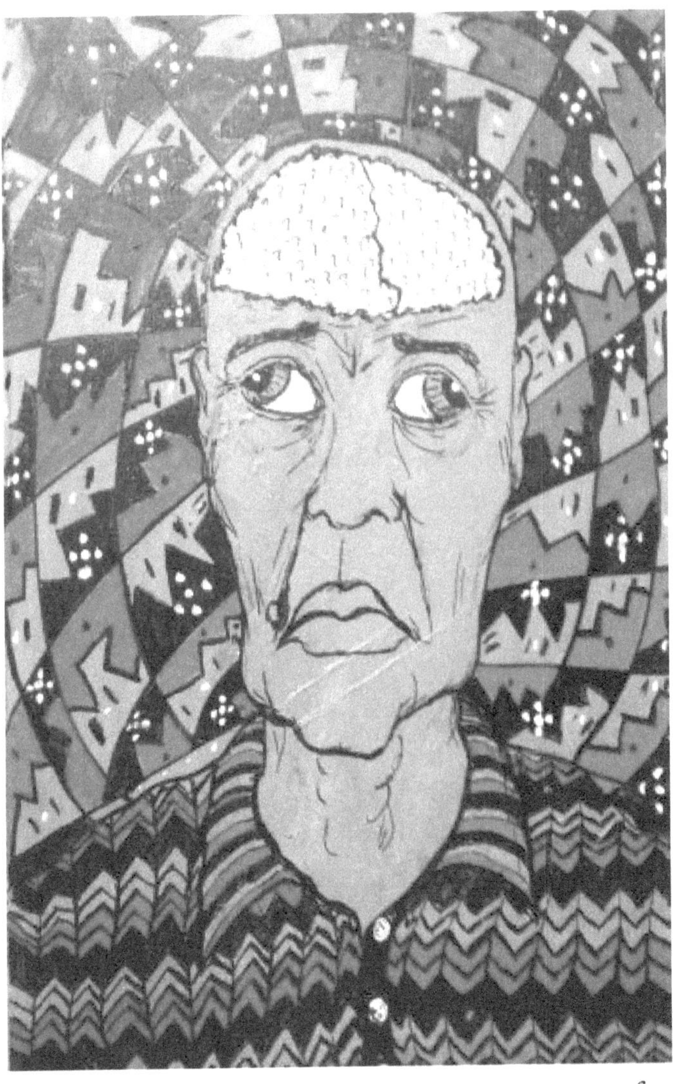

This book is controversial because it goes against some of our beliefs and the traditions of men. Many so-called Christians and Non-Christians may be offended or find fault with this book because of their perspective of biblical/scriptural contents. Many so-called black people and so-called white people may be offended because of the contents of this book because it may not support their theory of supremacy or entitlement. Many so-called Jews may be offended because this book may have a different perspective of the so-called chosen people than what is portrayed in the media.

Many so-called yellow (Asian), red (Native American), brown (Hispanic) people may be offended because of the lack of references about them in this book. Essentially, anyone who reads this book with a closed mind may be offended.

However, anyone who is capable of being objective and look at the facts, beliefs, and hypothesis presented

in this book will be able realize that this book was not designed to offend anyone.

If you are a bible believing Christian, it is my hope that I will present some information and perspectives about human beings and the bible that you may not have considered before. If you are a not a bible believing person it is still my hope that I will present some information and perspectives about human beings and the bible that you may not have considered before but I will know that you do not value what I believe is the Word of God.

I have spent most of my adult life being a master diplomat meaning that I strove to get along with people and not have conflict. I delayed completing this book because I knew that people could be offended and that went against my earthly personality. However, as I have matured in Christ I came to realize that it is impossible

to please everyone and that I will not be liked by everyone. Therefore, I do not have to answer to people, but at the end of my days my knees will bend before the Lord and my tongue will confess to the Lord. I do not want to be shamed in disobedience henceforth it does not matter if I sell one copy of this book to myself or one billion copies of this book to the world I must be obedient to that which I am called.

When I was working on my master's and doctorate degree's I learned about using scholarly and credible resources to validate and strengthen my assignments. I do believe in using credible and even scholarly resources however I had to take it a step further and evaluate who decides what is credible and not credible. There are a lot of agenda's in the world and we as human beings have been trained to disregard anything that may be labeled a conspiracy theory. Therefore, this

book does not regard nor disregard so-called conspiracy

theories, myths, folk tales, legends, or any other fancy label determined by the world. The basis of any theory or perspective will be bible and or scripturally based and examine how other sources may fill in the blanks. Insomuch, I have received a lot of attention from the evil thief who has been attempting and sometimes successfully distracting and delaying me from completing this book.

John 10:10 states, "The thief cometh not, but for to steal, and to kill, and to destroy: I am come that they might have life, and that they might have it more abundantly." The thief (Satan) comes to steal our joy, kill our dreams, and destroy our relationship with our Father in Heaven. The latter part (Destroy our relationship with our Father in Heaven) is a great deception because the thief does not have that kind of power. Nevertheless, if the thief can steal our joy and

kill our dreams he can make us as humans believe the lie.

Satan will try to steal our joy a number of ways through deception and distraction. First let's examine where real joy comes from. Real joy comes from love. God (The Father) is love and we come from God and are made in His image. Natural joy comes from loving your family especially your spouse, children, parents, and siblings.

In the Book of Genesis Satan sought to destroy the Adam and Eve's connection to their Heavenly Father by deceiving them to eat of the fruit they were commanded not to eat. When they disobeyed the command (committed sin) and their eyes were opened to the knowledge of good and evil they became ashamed and felt guilty and went and hid from their Father who loved them. The truth is God never stopped loving them but because of their sin. Adam

and Eve felt disconnected from God and lost because their joy stolen from them by Satan. However, Satan cannot come in and steal our joy from us, we open the door to Satan. He did not make Adam and Eve disobey God he planted the thought in Eve's head by making disobedience look appealing. Today sin still makes people feel disconnected from God and so people hide from God, ignore God, and some people convince themselves that God does not exist. Sin does not stop God from loving us but we act if though it does. Insomuch, the guilt from sin causes us to feel unworthy of God's love and we open the door to other sins and allow our joy to be stolen from us.

We as people open the door to have our joy to be stolen by Satan because of our curiosity and desires. Satan knows our weaknesses and how to deceive us.

Satan did not go to Adam to get him to eat of the fruit

because Adam was capable of standing against his tactics. One could speculate that Satan tried to deceive Adam before Eve was created and was unsuccessful however after Eve was created Satan knew how much Adam loved Eve and he knew that Adam would be weak to Eve. Satan appealed to Eve's curiosity and desire for knowledge to deceive her and he was successful. Eve gave the fruit to her husband and he did eat which caused the fall of mankind. Therefore, sin entered into the world and man gave his authority of the world over to Satan.

One might ask how man could give his earthly authority over to Satan. The answer is simple; sin is how man turned earthly authority over to Satan. Each time we sin we are in agreement with demons/angels of Satan and give them authority to act through us. Many people would like to comfort themselves and say that the devil made me do it. However, the truth is the Devil proposes an idea in our heads and we think about it then we act upon the thought.

Let's look in the Book of Genesis at the story of Cain and Abel. God knows our thoughts and sends messages through The Holy Ghost to speak to us prior to our inappropriate actions. The world has depicted this in the form of the good angel and the devil angel speaking to an individual before making a decision. In the case of Cain after becoming angry at God for rejecting his offering and jealous of his brother Abel for his offering being accepted God spoke directly to Cain prior to his actions. According to Genesis 4:6, "And the Lord said unto Cain, 'Why art thou wroth? and why is thy countenance fallen?'" God was essentially challenging Cain to dig deeper by truthfully examining his feelings and encouraging Cain to think positively instead of negatively.

In the next verse God warns Cain what could happen if he makes a better effort or what will happen if he stays negative. Genesis 4:7, "'If thou doest well, shalt thou not be accepted? and if thou doest not well, sin lieth at the door. And unto thee shall be his desire, and thou shalt rule over him.'" Henceforth, like in Cain's situation when we do well we (our spirit) will rule over sin (flesh) however when do not do well (our spirit) our sinful desires (flesh) will dominate us and give authority to Satan's demon angels to entangle us.

We must realize that we are at war and the battlefield is in our mind. God has given us free agency the ability to choose either good or evil. The term free agency is not found in the bible but it does mean that mankind is not forced to do things but have a choice.

The Book of Deuteronomy 30:19[1] states, "I call heaven and earth to record this day against you, that I have set before you: life and death, blessing and cursing:

---

1.   https://www.biblegateway.com/passage/?search=Deuteronomy+30:19&version=KJV

therefore choose life, that both thou and thy seed may live." Everything that we do on earth is recorded in heaven. However, we can choose life and be blessed.

When we choose Jesus Christ as our Lord and Savior we choose life. Those who reject Jesus Christ don not believe that He is the way to eternal life and therefore sometimes unknowingly choose death or sin which eventually leads to curses on earth. Another bible verse Joshua 24:15[2] states, "And if it seem evil unto you to serve the Lord, choose you this day whom ye will serve; whether the gods which your fathers served that were on the other side of the flood, or the gods of the

Amorites, in whose land ye dwell: but as for me and my house, we will serve the Lord." Therefore, in our minds we must choose between God's or Satan's side.

Many of us have enjoyed the pleasures of sin and rebelled against God. God's commands are designed

to keep our spirits stronger than our flesh. Sin gives power to the flesh which creates habits and addictions. Those addictions combined with our selfishness form an alliance against God and become a god in our lives. Those of us who can still have compassion for others and feel remorse for sinning sometimes try to keep enough God to get to heaven but enough Satan to enjoy the flesh. When we try to keep both God and Satan we become double minded. Satan tries to get mankind to serve and worship money or mammon.

We have to know that Satan does not care if we serve him directly or not as long as he can get us to worship anything other than God. Matthew 6:24 states, "No man can serve two masters: for either he will hate the one, and love the other; or else he will hold to the one, and despise the other. Ye cannot serve God and mammon."

Some Christians secretly despise God because they

want to fulfill their fleshly desires and eventually make themselves out to be hypocrites and double minded. James 1: 8 states, "A double

---

2.   https://www.biblegateway.com/passage/?search=Joshua+24:15&version=KJV

minded man is unstable in all his ways." Fortunately, God's grace and the blood of Jesus Christ is sufficient for our fleshly weaknesses and will provide the strength that we need to overcome our personal struggles in the flesh.

The bible tells us that we can transform our hearts and minds by confessing our sins to God and humbly submitting ourselves to Him. James 4:7 states, "Submit yourselves therefore to God. Resist the devil, and he will flee from you." We have to resist the devil (Satan) and his temptations to sin. We have to become strong in the mind and spirit and seek God through his word (scripture), prayer (communicating with God), and fasting (denying the flesh).

James 4:8 states, "Draw nigh to God, and he will draw nigh to you. Cleanse your hands, ye sinners; and purify your hearts, ye double minded." We are not victims because we chose what we do. However, if we are aware of Satan's tactics we can prevent him from becoming double-minded and guard against Satan stealing our joy, killing our dreams, and destroying our relationship with our Father in Heaven.

Steal		Kill		Destroy	
Joy for Life		**Hope and Dreams for a better Future**		**Relationship with the Father**	
Natural Replacement		**Natural Replacement**		**Natural Replacement**	
		Seek purpose	Self-doubt		
		Make Plans	Guilt		
	Crave Alcohol	Create things	Accept Defeat	Love the Father	
Love Family	Crave being High	Build things	Settle for how things are	Honor the Father	Hide from the Father
Love Spouse	Crave Nicotine	Help others	Suicidal Thoughts	Please the Father	Ignore the Father
Love Children	Crave Narcotics	Experience Life	Murder Thoughts	Serve the Father	Deny the Father
Love Neighbor	Crave Fornication	Learn Things	Blame others	Represent the Father	Resist the Father
Love Nature	Crave Adultery	Teach others	Negativity	Trust the Father	Rebel against the Father
Love to Laugh	Crave Pornography	Assist others	Put self down		Hate the Father
Love Clean Fun	Crave Gossip		Put others down		
Love to Help	Crave Drama		Jealousy		
Love to Serve	Crave Revenge		Sabotage		
Love Good Works	Crave to Cause Pain		Start Chaos		
Love to do Good			Enjoy others misfortune		

Steal	Kill	Destroy
You must fight to keep your joy. If you keep your joy you will keep your hope & dreams will stay alive as well as a love relationship with The Father. If you don't fight to keep your joy you will lose it and then lose your hope and dreams and tarnish your relationship with The Father.	If you keep your joy you can have faith in God and hope for a better future. When your joy has been stolen you fill them with Satan's replacements and lose your faith in God and have	You have faith in God and feel good about your salvation because of your relationship You don't have confidence in your relationship with God. You either think you are unworthy of salvation, you are prideful, selfish and disregard God, or you intentionally work against God.

with God.

Chapter Two: God's Purpose for Mankind and Sex

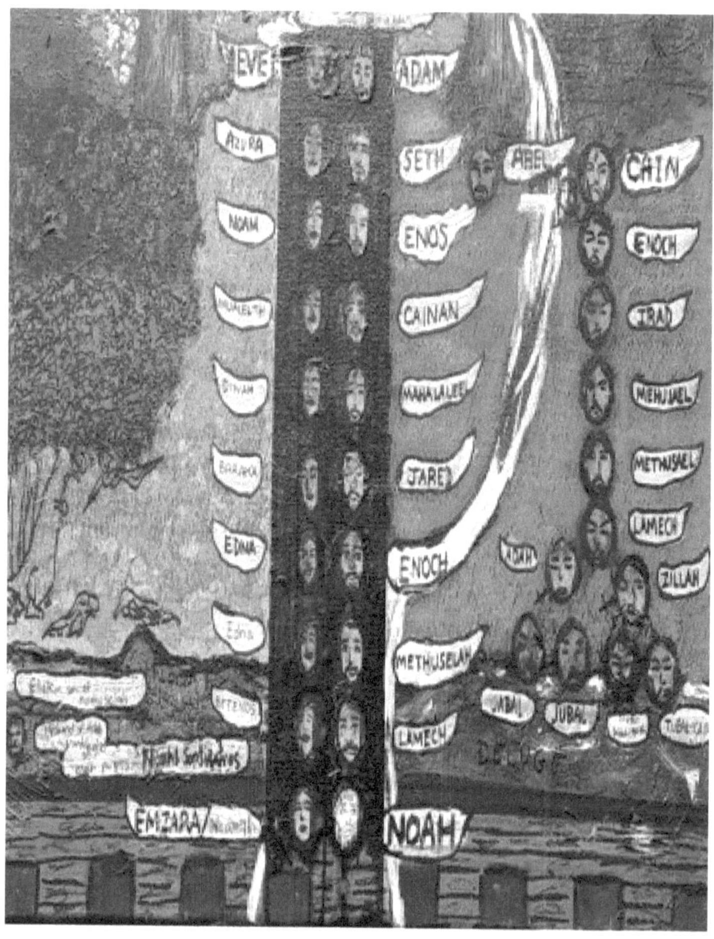

The image above is 1/6th of the painting "From Adam to Jesus" by The Minister Artist.

You must decide if you believe in the "Holy Bible", "The Big Bang Theory", "The Theory of Evolution" or none of the above. If you believe the bible as I do, then you accept the biblical origins of Adam and Eve.

Please notice, according to the bible, man is both spirit and flesh, and the man's spirit was created first. Genesis 1:26, "And God said, 'Let us make man in our image, after our likeness: and let them have dominion over the fish of the sea, and over the fowl of the air, and over the cattle, and over all the earth, and over every creeping thing that creepeth upon the earth.'" Genesis 26 is where man's spirit was created and given authority prior to coming to earth.

Also notice that God said, 'let us make man in our image.' Who are (the let us) they are referring too?

I choose to believe that "us" is The Father (God/Yah),

The Son (Jesus Christ/ Messiah/Yeshua), and The Holy Ghost/ Holy Spirit. We could also conclude that

all of our spirits were created in heaven before we come to earth in wait for a body in a mother's womb. Henceforth, let's continue with the next scripture.

Genesis 1:27 states, "So God created man in his own image, in the image of God created he him; male and female created he them." Therefore, Genesis 1:27 tells us that God decided in Heaven who is male and who is female. Prior to entering our mother's earthly womb, we are declared by God what sex we are. We also know that our spirit is perfect because we are created in the image of God.

Today we live in a world where man thinks that God makes mistakes and that individuals know better than God if they should be male or female. The rest of Genesis Chapter 1 commanded men and women to have sex and to have children to replenish the earth.

God blessed men and women with herbs and fruit

bearing trees for nourishment and gave them authority over all the creatures of the air, sea, and land. God's plan was set prior to the creation of the earthly body of mankind. Insomuch, in Genesis Chapter 2 God had planted the seeds in the field but held back the rain for the seeds to grow until He created and earthly man.

According to Genesis 2, "And the Lord God formed man of the dust of the ground, and breathed into his nostrils the breath of life; and man became a living soul." Therefore, the body (flesh) of man comes from the dust of the ground (dirt) and water. Yes—water. In Genesis 2:6 it states, "But there went up a mist from the earth, and watered the whole face of the ground." Therefore, if God watered the earth prior to making man, there is water in the body of man. Science

tells us that the human body is greater than 50 percent water.

God create the earthly body for man's spirit and

when the Lord God breathed unto the earthly body breathed His life unto the body man became a living soul which is both spirit and flesh. God created man to work on the earth. God gave man free reign upon the earth and gave him commandments about what he could eat from and the one tree of knowledge of good and evil which he should not eat from. Man obeyed all of God's commands without any struggle.

However, God noticed that it was not good for man to be alone in Genesis 2:18, so God decided it was time for a female spirit to come to earth. Genesis 2:21, "And the Lord God caused a deep sleep to fall upon Adam, and he slept: and he took one of his ribs, and closed up the flesh instead thereof." Henceforth, God performed the first surgery and genetically created a new life in His laboratory which is the earth.

Genesis 2:19, "And the rib, which the Lord God

had taken from man, made he a woman, and brought her unto the man." God created a helpmeet for man because he needed help. God entrusted Adam with many responsibilities (including naming all the animals) which he was able to do without interference but now that the bulk of the initial work was complete it was time for the next phase. Adam called the female a woman because she came out of him and was bone of his bones and flesh of his flesh. It was God's purpose for them to be husband and wife and father and mother. "Therefore, shall a man leave his father and his mother, and shall cleave unto his wife: and they shall be one flesh" (Genesis 2:24).

The Lord God made everything beautiful and there was nothing shameful including the nudity of man and woman. Shame did not enter the world until the serpent (Satan/The Devil) came into the scene. I believe that the serpent knew that he could not get Adam to break

God's commands. Perhaps the serpent already tried and failed to get Adam to betray God but the serpent knew that man's weakness was the woman. He knew if he could smooth talk the woman that he could get man to follow. The serpent knew just how to take the truth and mix it with a lie to deceive the woman who became known as Eve. The serpent appealed to the woman's desire to be wise by gaining knowledge and power to be a god. However, she did not have the wisdom to see through the serpents plan nor have an understanding of the potential consequences of disobeying God.

Adam—as a man—was weak when it came to Eve, and I believe that he chose to eat the fruit so he would not be without Eve, even though he knew he was disobeying God.

I believe that the events of Genesis Chapter 3 established that man's fleshly desire for a woman is

stronger than his desire to obey God. Today when men and women struggle in fleshly things such as pornography it is stronger than their desire to obey God. Fortunately, for us God already had a plan in place to save us from our fleshly desires in the form of His Son. Most people who chose to read this book are familiar with the shame that Adam and Eve shared when their knowledge of good and evil kicked in and the realized they were naked and tried to hide from God. Most people reading this book are familiar with the consequences that Adam, Eve, and the serpent received as a result of breaking God's commandment not to eat of the Tree of Knowledge. The bible is so true to this day.

God told Eve that because of her part of the disobedience act that she would have pain in child birth.

Of course women to this day have different degrees

of pain in child birth. Adam received a harsh penalty of

having to work hard by sweating to till the ground to be able to eat. Today there are various jobs in which all men do not have to farm the land yet man does not eat without tilling the ground to bear food to eat.

Therefore, the bible is true because man needs to work to eat. Even in role reversal if a man is living off of a woman she is either working or has an income through a system created by man that she is able to provide food to eat.

Role reversal is another topic but was only mentioned to make the point that the bible is true even in today's culture. It is also funny how the woman blamed the serpent and the man blamed the woman and how people shift blame in our world today. Today many people still do not want to accept blame for their faults and shortcomings which is actually the beginning

of healing and overcoming. Henceforce, the

consequence of the serpent after the woman confessed and blamed the serpent for her failure to obey needs to be discussed further.

Genesis 3:14 states, "And the Lord God said unto the serpent, 'Because thou hast done this, thou art cursed above all cattle, and above every beast of the field; upon thy belly shalt thou go, and dust shalt thou eat all the days of thy life.'" I believe that the spirit of Satan entered unto a serpent which was able to walk and talk during and before the incident in the Garden of Eden. When God cursed the serpent above all cattle and every beast of the field to go through life upon its belly, I envision a metamorphic change in which the Satan is no longer able to talk or walk through the serpent. Nevertheless, serpents, snakes, vipers, and any other name will always be associated with Satan.

The next verse in Genesis 3:15 is often overlooked

because it is not understood by many people.

Genesis 3:15 states: And I will put enmity between thee and the woman, and between thy seed and her seed; it shall bruise thy head, and thou shalt bruise his heel. The word enmity derives from the word enemy meaning hostile, dislike, or ill will towards something or someone. Therefore, the serpent and the woman are supposed to hate each other. Ironically, you will see some female entertainers holding snakes in their performances when they are supposed to hate each other.

The unanswered question, who is the serpent's seed and who is the woman's seed? Is this a physical statement or a spiritual statement from God? I propose this hypothesis; even though the serpent does not have a known physical seed other than assuming physical serpents/snakes and we know that the woman continually gives physical birth to children. I submit

the ideology that the serpent's seed is physical (earthly/worldly) and the woman's seed is spiritual (heavenly). We know that Satan appeals to mankind's flesh which is physical and earthly. We also know that the woman gives birth to spiritual beings inside the flesh. The woman is the connection of life between the heavenly realms and the earth. The serpent/Satan continually entices mankind through sex, power, fame, and fortune. Satan is a liar, deceiver, distracter, manipulator, and controller over men whom he tries to get mankind addicted to anything besides God. Through the woman are born disciples, preachers, teachers, pastors, prophets, apostles, and the Messiah.

Later in the Book of Genesis it talks about twins born which are two nations one which is Jacob/Israel and the other is Esau/Edom. Jacob who was not perfect in the flesh valued the spiritual promises of God, and Esau, who also was not perfect, valued the

earthly and worldly things and did not value God. I do not believe that it is possible to have any pure seeded people. Even our Lord and

Savior had various blood lines in his DNA. The savior had so called forbidden Canaanite blood, Moabite blood, and who knows what else in his genealogy. I do not believe that it was an accident that the New Testament started off in Matthew Chapter One with the genealogy of Jesus. It would be difficult to find someone of pure Edomites blood or pure Israelites blood. Nevertheless, it is rumored there are 13 families that marry within the family to keep the purity of the bloodline and be of the serpent's seed.

It is also rumored that the 13 families are the elite controlling families which are less than 1% of the world's population, but have the majority of the world's wealth. This is another conversation. If Esau or Edom

represents the serpent's seed and Jacob or Israel represents the woman's seed, then the rest of the bible makes sense.

Geneses 27 tells us that Esau wanted to kill Jacob after receiving his father's blessing but he waited for his father to die first not to cause him pain in life. Notice how the mother favored Jacob and helped him to deceive her husband and his father to receive the much valued spiritual blessing. Esau only sought to please his flesh and his hunting of venison pleased his father's flesh. The bible says in Malachi 1:3 that the Lord hated Esau and that Edom would come to ruin.

Romans 9:13 As it is written, Jacob have I loved, but Esau have I hated. Jacob and Esau were long dead and gone when the books of Malachi and Romans were written and the DNA of their off spring would be thoroughly mixed with other nations; therefore, it would be difficult to depict a pure DNA. Although, the

bible and other ancient books say that Edom lived in the mountains, before coming down from the mountains. Again that is another topic. Therefore, I propose that Esau represents the serpent's fleshly seed and Israel represents the woman's spiritual seed.

Esau (serpent seed) is in control of the world today and is oppressing Israel (woman seed) at every opportunity. Genesis said that serpent would bite the heel of the woman's seed but the woman's seed will bruise the head of the serpent's seed. The woman's seed has some extremely sore heels right now but when Jesus/ Yeshua Christ/Messiah returns the head of the serpent will be bruised forever. These are just a few things we have learned about the flesh and God's purpose for mankind from the book of Genesis. God created the spirits of men and women before giving

them a fleshly body. God created fleshly body out of

the dust of the earth. God created Eve to be Adam's wife and helpmeet.

God created men and woman to have sex and bring forth children to populate the earth. For most people the sexual intercourse is pleasurable. However, women have various degrees of pain during child birth.

Satan's goal consists of corrupting mankind by tempting and tricking mankind to misuse their bodies against God's purpose.

I propose the following ideology regarding the difference between sin and an abomination. Sin is the act of misusing the natural God given desires for selfish purposes. For instance, fornication is having sex without being married. Sexual desires are natural but it

goes against God's purpose for sex because He wants the man and woman to be married. Adultery is a sin because it violates the God ordained union between a man and woman with an outside party. However, the

bible calls man laying with man like a woman an abomination and bestiality confusion. An abomination is the act of using selfish desires for unnatural acts. This statement may upset some people because I stated that it was unnatural but what I am really saying is that a man having sex with a man cannot produce a natural child and the same for a woman with a woman cannot produce a natural child. Same sex relationships can only obtain children through adoption, previous heterosexual encounter, or a surrogate mother. Mankind would eventually cease to exist if heterosexual encounters were abolished.

Test tube surrogacy is not natural child conception and it still takes the seed of a man to be implanted into the egg of a woman. Leviticus 18:22 states: Thou shalt not lie with mankind, as with womankind: it is an abomination. A human being having sex with an

animal cannot produce a human child. Animals do not sexually violate humans but humans can violate or entice animals. God did not randomly give us commandments and laws because He felt like it.

Each commandment has a purpose to help keep us on track to fulfill our pre-ordained destiny.

Before men and women are born to their earthly parents they were commandment to be fruitful and multiply. Genesis 1: 27 states: So God created man in his own image, in the image of God created he him; male and female created he them. This verse talks about what took place in heaven because Adam was not formed until chapter 2. Genesis 1: 28 states: And God blessed them, and God said unto them, "Be fruitful, and multiply, and replenish the earth, and subdue it: and have dominion over the fish of the sea, and over the fowl of the air, and over every living thing that moveth upon the earth." God gave a commandment to

be fruitful and multiple before the bodies of the first man and woman were created on earth. God also gave man authority over the creatures of the earth to keep the natural order. Insomuch, going against God's natural order by any mistreatment or perversion of God's purpose is either a sin or an abomination. I am not judging anyone because it is not my place nor desire but I am simply sharing what the scriptures say and offer my perspective of them.

Chapter Three: Power of Women over the Lust Men and Angels

Angels coming to Earth from Heaven
by The Minister Artist

In the book of Genesis, we learned how the serpent/Satan tricked Eve unto partaking of the forbidden fruit then proceeded to convince her husband Adam to partake as well. The partaking of the fruit from the first couple has become known as the fall. Satan used Eve to get Adam to fall from the grace of God. Satan has not stopped using women to get men to fall. However, before I continue talking about how men fell through the influence of women let's talk about how the angels/sons of God fell to the beauty of women.

According to the Book of Enoch before the flood there were a group of fallen angels that came to earth and interacted with the women on earth. Many traditional scholars don't accept the Book of Enoch as scripture and say that it is not inspired. Some say they believe the Book of Enoch is fictitious. I suggest that

you listen to the evidence with an open mind and

decide for yourself what you believe. Nevertheless, let's look at what takes place before the fallen angels which consist of the children of Adam and Eve. My approach consists of using what the bible tells us and filling in the blanks with non-canonized ancient books. For instance, some scholars say that the sons of God mentioned in Genesis 6 are the fallen angels. Henceforth, Genesis 6:2 states: That the sons of God saw the daughters of men that they were fair; and they took them wives of all which they chose.

If the sons of God are fallen angels this helps Genesis 6 make a lot of sense. The angels were drawn away by the fairness/beauty of women and left their first estate to cohabitate with women of earth and flesh. These angels chose to defy and sin against God. Some may argue that angels can't mix in with people or take human form. Some may say that angels would never

sin against God. Well I am here to tell you that the bible says differently. Jude 1:6 and the angels which kept not their first estate, but left their own habitation, he hath reserved in everlasting chains under darkness unto the judgment of the great day. Hell was created for the angels who disobeyed what God created them to do and the fallen angels (sons of God) left their home in heaven to be with women will be judged with everlasting punishment. These angels gave into fornication and went after strange flesh. Strange flesh is nonhuman flesh such as animals or bestiality. Insomuch, Jude 1:7 states: Even as Sodom and Gomorrah, and the cities about them in like manner, giving themselves over to fornication, and going after strange flesh, are set forth for an example, suffering the vengeance of eternal fire.

Many people reading this book are familiar with the story of Sodom and Gomorrah. According to

Genesis 19:1, And there came two angels to Sodom at even; and Lot sat in the gate of Sodom: and Lot seeing them rose up to meet them; and he bowed himself with his face toward the ground. The two angels looked like men in flesh. The men of Sodom young and old seen the two men with Lot and they wanted to have sex with them. Genesis 19:5 and they called unto Lot, and said unto him, where are the men which came in to thee this night? Bring them out unto us, that we may know them. The men of Sodom surrounded lot's house and demanded that the men came outside they could rape them. If the two angels did not look like humans in the flesh the men of Sodom would not desire them. Lot even offered his two virgin daughters but the men were homosexual and they did not desire women. (This is another topic). The point of this story was to show that the bible says that angels can take the form of human

beings. Furthermore, the angels are mentioned in the New Testament regarding women.

First Corinthians chapter 11 talks about how women were created for men however man is not without the woman and the woman is not without the man. 1 Corinthians 11:10 states: For this cause ought the woman to have power on her head because of the angels. What does that verse really mean? Initially when I read this I thought of a veil or hat to show reverence to the angels. However, we are to revere God not the angels. We are to respect angels as workers and messengers of God. I believe that a woman ought to have power over her head is to be married and have the authority of her husband over her not as her boss but her partner and mate. Upon reading the verse again in the King

James Version and other older bible versions it comes across to me that the bible is saying beware of certain angels. Angels evidently have free will just as

humans do and they will be judged accordingly just as humans will. Matthew 22:30 and Mark 12:25 tell us that angels of heaven do not marry. God did not create angels to marry. However, angels in a fallen state outside of heaven have the ability to do as men do and much more.

Let's revisit Genesis 6:1-2 and compare it the Book of Enoch VI: 1-2. Genesis 6:1 states: And it came to pass, when men began to multiply on the face of the earth, and daughters were born unto them. The Book of Enoch VI: 1states: And it came to pass when the children of men had multiplied that in those days were born unto them beautiful and comely daughters.

Both books are recognizing that mankind has multiplied on the earth and daughters were born.

Genesis 6: 2 states: That the sons of God saw the daughters of men that they were fair; and they took

them wives of all which they chose. The Book of Enoch VI: 2 states: And the angels, the children of the heaven, saw and lusted after them, and said to one another: 'Come, let us choose us wives from among the children of men and beget us children. The King James Version said sons of God and The Book of Enoch said the angels of heaven. However, the texts are similar and The Book of Enoch stated that the angels of heaven lusted after the women and made ungodly plans to take them as wives and have children with them. Notice even the angels who chose to disobey God still valued

wives and children before the greater perversions. Henceforth, let's further examine the Book of Enoch.

The book of Enoch continues by naming some of the angels which is not the focal point of this book.

However, the angels made an agreement they would stick together and their leader, Semjaza, would not take responsibility by himself for their transgression against

God. The Book of Enoch VI: 6 And they were in all two hundred; who descended [in the days] of Jared on the summit of Mount Hermon, and they called it Mount Hermon, because they had sworn and bound themselves by mutual imprecations upon it. Notice that they descended in the days of Jared who is the 6th generation from Adam and the father of Enoch. The people on earth had been multiplying for hundreds of years by this time. Therefore, these are not the angels that transgressed with Lucifer/Satan/ Serpent/The Dragon mentioned in The Book of Revelations and Isaiah. These angels witnessed the war in heaven and either fought with Michael against Satan and his angels or observed as bystanders. Either way they were fully aware there would be a consequence for their choice to disobey God. How powerful is a beautiful woman that even angels of heaven chose to disobey God? It makes

me wonder if we as mere human men even have a chance to be obedient to God. It also makes me think about how thrilling it is to sin. Sinning is fun until you have a conscience for God. Since humans are both spirit and flesh we struggle in the mind if we should obey our spirit or flesh. However, the fallen angels brought mankind some things to persuade people to obey only the flesh.

The fallen angels were from heaven and by cohabitating with earthly women with human flesh they defile themselves. The Book of Enoch VII: 1states: And all the others together with them took unto themselves wives, and each chose for himself one, and they began to go in unto them and to defile themselves with them, and they taught them charms and enchantments, and the cutting of roots, and made them acquainted with plants. The fallen angels brought witchcraft to the women of earth. Prior to the fallen angels, the people of earth dealt with the rebellion of Cain and his offspring but now because of the angels' wickedness was taken to another level to corrupt the people of earth. The Book of Enoch VII: 2 states: And they became pregnant, and they bare great giants, whose height was three thousand ells. If the height measurement is true which is hard for my human mind to fathom one ell is equivalent to 3.75 feet. That would make the giants 11,250 feet. That height would be greater than 7 times the height of the Sears Tower in Chicago. However, if the giants grew to be anywhere from 30 to 60 feet tall or taller according to Dr. Stephen Pidgen which I believe would be more likely especially considering Giant bones that were discovered but disappeared after the Smithsonian showed up. Mortal men would not have been able to sustain them and eventually the giants would have turned against

men and began to devour them. The book of Enoch VII: 5 states: And they began to sin against birds, and beasts, and reptiles, and fish, and to devour one another's flesh, and drink the blood. Angels choosing to sin against the animals means they began to have sex with animals and they impregnated beast and created hybrid creatures. Likewise, Jude 1:7 mentioned that the angels went after strange flesh. Going after strange flesh means they were having sex with animals. Thereunto, let's examine some so called mythological creatures mentioned in the bible.

We have been programmed to believe that some creatures were mythological or fairy tales for entertainment purposes. However, I had to ask myself if I believed the bible to be the word of God, then I must accept what the bible says. I also had to ask myself since I believe the bible to the word of God, then why would certain creatures that we do not see

on earth anymore exist in the bible. Furthermore, if they existed in the bible then they must have been real. The bible also mentions how angels took human formed and appeared as human to other humans like in the story of Sodom and Gomorrah.

A satyr is a combination of a human looking man and a goat. The Satyr is mentioned in Isaiah 13:24 and Isaiah 34:14 in the King James Version. There are some critics of the King James Version and bible critics that will say that Satyrs are mythical. The Amplified Bible mentions a Satyr as a goat demon in 2Chronicles 11:15. The 1599 Geneva Bible uses the same verses in Isaiah as the King James Version but many bibles do not translate the word Satyr at all. Some biblical versions phrase Isaiah 13:24 for example the (NIV)

New International Version and the (NLT) New Living Translation use wild goats in place of Satyr.

The NIV says the wild goats will leap out and the NLT says and wild goats will go there to dance. Isaiah 13: 24 KJV says and Satyrs shall dance there. Henceforth, there are other beast mentioned in the bible that may or may not be hybrids but considered mythological.

The creature unicorn was mentioned 9 times in the KJV Bible, 10 times in the 1599 Geneva Bible, 10 times in the Wycliffe Bible, but 0 times in the NIV & NLT Bibles. Leviathan is mentioned 4 times in the KJV Bible, 5 times in the 1599 Geneva Bible, 5 times in the Wycliffe Bible, 6 times in the NIV Bible, and 8 times in the NLT Bible. I must admit that the different bible translations are confusing to me because it seems that each would have similar translations whether they are

translating Hebrew, Aramaic, or Greek to English. There appears to be an agenda to include or exclude things from the bible. Now my feelings of confusion,

has changed to fear for the bible translators because of the book of Revelations which states in KJV version: 22: 18-19 For I testify unto every man that heareth the words of the prophecy of this book, if any man shall add unto these things, God shall add unto him the plagues that are written in this book: And if any man shall take away from the words of the book of this prophecy, God shall take away his part out of the book of life, and out of the holy city, and from the things which are written in this book. Insomuch, if there is indeed a conspiracy let's consider other popular either mystical or extinct creatures.

The book of Enoch stated angels began to sin against birds, and beasts, and reptiles, and fish, and to devour one another's flesh, and drink the blood. Horus the Egyptian God is depicted with the head of a falcon (bird) body of a man, Siren is half bird half woman who

lured sailors with her singing voice, Vampires and Dracula that can transform into flying bats and drink blood, Centaur has the upper body of a man and lower body of a horse (beast), Sphinx has the upper body of a man and lower body of a lion (beast), Pan has the body of a man but horns and legs of a goat (beast), Baphomet has the head of a goat and a human body with male and female features (beast), Meduza is a woman depicted with snake features that can kill on sight, people with reptilian eyes that change and blink differently, and one of the most popular hybrids are mermaids which are half woman and half fish.

The previously listed are some of the most popular hybrid creatures today but are just a fraction of a list of so called mythical creatures. I do not believe that every previously mentioned creature is real but I do believe what the bible and book of Enoch says is true that it would not be hard for me to perceive the possibility

that hybrid creatures actually existed. Today there are hidden science labs doing all kinds of experiments unknown to the public. There are probably human hybrids living among us without our knowledge. One of my favorite YouTube pastors the late great Stephen Darby of Destined Ministries talked about how laws are being passed when we are distracted by other events in the world.

He also spoke about the days of Noah when hybrids were common on earth. Dr. Eugene Chen of San Jose Bible Baptist Church who is strictly King James Version has spoken of hybrids and giants on You Tube. Rob Skiba and many other teachers/preachers who are talking about the Nephillim and hybrid creatures on YouTube from a variety of so called races and nationalities that I believe that we need to open our eyes to the possibilities or realities. It would be easy

for me to believe that human hybrids and other hybrids are on the earth today. Hollywood's goal is to make money, sell propaganda, and tell a story. Even though a movie or show may be fiction Hollywood, gets its story line from a variety of sources that become a mixture of rumors, superstitions, and truth. Truth can be stranger than fiction. One of Satan's ploys is to mix a lie with the truth to be deceitful. Another ploy by Satan is to hide the truth in plain sight. He will make things so obvious you will either not see it or not believe it. Insomuch, many people will brush the claim off that angels came to earth and cohabitated with human women and even for those who accept cohabitation with women may reject fallen angels lying with animals.

I am asking for people to read the scriptures for themselves. Pray about it and ask the Holy Ghost/Spirit for guidance regarding what is written in this book. I must say that this is not as important as

giving your life to God by accepting Jesus Christ as your Lord and Savior. However, it is important to learn the truth for yourself along with confirmation to your spirit. According to the book of Jubilees Noah died in the year (1659 AM). It was 29 years (1688 AM) later when Ham and his sons dispersed from the land of Shinar to occupy the portion of land they were to occupy. This was after the incident of the Tower of Babel. Jubilees 10: 29 states: And Canaan saw the land of Lebanon to the river of Egypt, that it was very good, and he went not into the land of his inheritance to the west (that is to) the sea, and he dwelt in the land of Lebanon, eastward and westward from the border of Jordan and from the border of the sea.

Ham Canaan's father along with two of his brothers Cush (Ethiopia) and Mizriam (Egypt) told Canaan not to dwell in Shem's land but he did it anyway.

Jubilees 10:32 states: Cursed art thou, and cursed shalt thou be beyond all the sons of Noah, by the curse by which we bound ourselves by an oath in the presence of the holy judge, and in the presence of Noah our father.' Therefore, Noah had revelation and prophesied that Canaan would take this land because it did not happen until 29 years after his death according to the book of Jubilees.

Something strange was going on in the days of Noah after the flood. However, prior to the flood there was a prophecy in Genesis 6. Genesis 6:4 states: There were giants in the earth in those days; and also after that, when the sons of God came in unto the daughters of men, and they bare children to them, the same became mighty men which were of old, men of renown. The NIV, AMP, and some other biblical texts called the giants the Nephillim. The Nephillim/Giants are the off spring of the sons of God (Fallen Angels) mating with

human women. However, what is strange and confusing is the statement that there were giants/Nephillim earth those days and also after that.

The bible stated in Genesis 7:21: And all flesh died that moved upon the earth, both of fowl, and of cattle, and of beast, and of every creeping thing that creepeth upon the earth, and every man. That verse gives you the impression that every creature died except those that were on the ark. However, look again at the next verse Genesis 7:22 which states: All in whose nostrils was the

breath of life, of all that was in the dry land, died, all that were on the dry ground died. Again the next verse Genesis 7:23 states: And every living substance was destroyed which was upon the face of the ground, both man, and cattle, and the creeping things, and the fowl of the heaven; and they were destroyed from the earth: and Noah only remained alive, and they that were with

him in the ark. The three previous verses were a huge clue that the creatures that could live in the water did not die. Henceforth, aquatic creatures were not affected by the flood because water is their natural habitat.

In reference to the fallen angels they did not only cohabitate with earthly women but also animals. The Book of Enoch VII: 5 states: And they began to sin against birds, and beasts, and reptiles, and fish. The angel off spring with birds and beast would have died in the flood but some of the reptile off spring and all of the fish off spring would have survived the flood. I can't help but to think of mermaids. I have seen more than one movie where mermaids can have legs temporarily to walk on dry land. Movies such as "Splash" with the actress Daryl Hannah is a fictional movie. However, what if some of the folklore that is used to create movies are true. That would mean that mermaids are real and can cohabitate with men post

flood. Many sailors over the centuries have claimed to have seen mermaids. Christopher Columbus and his crew claimed to have seen mermaids. However, the historians claimed that he really seen manatees. My issue historians could not possibly know what Columbus seen. They were not there on that day in 1493. Just because manatees were found in the area where Columbus sailed does not prove that is what Columbus saw. If you search the internet you will see a variety of images regarding mermaids. Some images look like imposters (fake) or photo shopped and some seem realistic. Insomuch, I believe there is a conspiracy to keep people from knowing the truth.

In our culture today we have been brainwashed

to ignore any conspiracy theory. We have been condition to ignore or belittle anything that does not fit in our way of thinking. We ignore certain facts and go

with the flow of the popular majority or the propaganda that has been presented to us. One such conspiracy is there is an organization that sweeps through and retrieves strange findings that are not easily explained to the general public. There are photographs of what looks like to be dead mermaids washed ashore but people don't have access to research the findings.

Chapter Four: After the Ark

Who are Noah's Descendants?

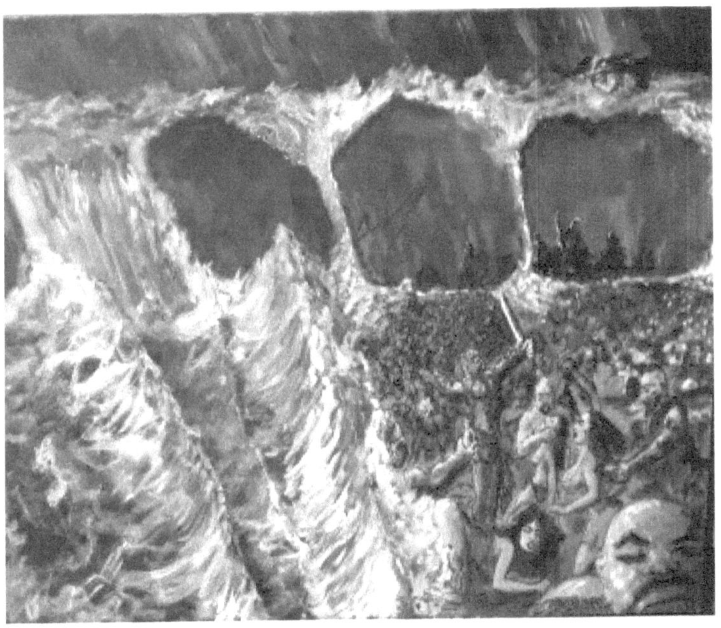

Blood the Flood
The Days of Noah by the Minister Artist

After the Flood
Uncovered Drunken Nakedness in the Tent
by the Minister Artist

One of my most troubling areas in the bible consist of why did Noah get so angry at his son Ham because he seen his nakedness but instead of cursing Ham he cursed Ham's son Canaan which is also Noah's grandson. The first thought is to take the bible at face value which is Noah felt disrespected by his son Ham. However, Noah feeling disrespected would not explain why Noah cursed Canaan. Some believe that Ham had sex with Noah's wife which would also be Ham's mother and had Canaan as a result of incest. This theory is based upon Leviticus 18:8 which states: The nakedness of thy father's wife shalt thou not uncover: it is thy father's nakedness. Even though I understand the rationale I still find this theory unlikely for a variety of reasons. First, Ham had a wife and he had four sons by

her and there was no need to be so desperate to sleep

with or rape your own mother. Secondly, Ham's mom

would not be so weak to have sex with her youngest son especially with her husband being alive. Third, Ham had to older brothers who would have caused Ham physical harm up to killing him for sleeping with their mother. Lastly, there are various theories to demonize Ham since he is believed to be the father of African nations to justify slavery.

Some people still refer to the incident as the curse of Ham even though the bible clearly states Canaan was cursed. Worse, is the tale that some people believe that Ham raped and sodomized his father Noah. Another story has Ham castrating his father so he would not be able to have more children so he would not have to split his inheritance of the earth with more siblings. I believe the above demonization of Ham was ridiculous and unmerited. I also do not believe that Ham merely seeing his father naked was enough to make Noah that angry. We have to use common sense and realize that

people, regardless of the time period are generally the same and no parent would get that angry over their child seeing them naked. Therefore, I will offer you what I believe the reason for Noah's anger and I will use scripture to support my belief.

Genesis Chapter 9 tells us that Noah planted a vineyard and made some wine and he drank it until he was drunk. Genesis 9:21 states: And he drank of the wine, and was drunken; and he was uncovered within his tent. Notice, that Noah is the (he) that was uncovered. Now let's examine Leviticus 18:6 None of you shall approach to any that is near of kin to him, to uncover their nakedness: I am the Lord. This means, do not have sex with a near kinsman. The word uncover means have sex. Genesis 9:22 states: And Ham, the father of Canaan, saw the nakedness of his

father, and told his two brethren without. The verse

said that Ham saw the nakedness of his father. It did not say that Ham uncovered the nakedness of his father. Let's revisit Leviticus 18:8 which states: The nakedness of thy father's wife shalt thou not uncover: it is thy father's nakedness. That does mean that the father's nakedness is his wife. Do not have sex with your father's wife. The bible never places Ham inside the tent. Noah was inside the tent. A book called "The Legend of the Jews" states that: In his drunken condition Noah betook himself to the tent of his wife.

Noah was having drunken sex with his wife and Ham saw them and probably watched them until they stopped and fell asleep. Then Ham went and told his brothers what he saw. Ham's brothers were not amused and respectfully covered them by walking backwards with a blanket. Noah possibly seen or felt Ham's presence but he was very much into his wife at the time. Those of us who are married or have been guilty

of fornication can relate to being very much into the moment. Most of us can also relate to the man falling asleep shortly afterwards. Therefore, I am proclaiming that Noah's anger at his son Ham came from him seeing or watching his parents have drunken sex which is voyeurism a form of pornography. However, that does not explain why Noah cursed Canaan and not Ham.

First of all, Noah could not curse Ham because God had blessed him. Genesis 9: 1 states: And God blessed Noah and his sons, and said unto them, "Be fruitful, and multiply, and replenish the earth." Noah could not undo the blessing upon Ham like Isaac could not undo the blessing upon Jacob that was meant for Esau once it was given even though he was deceived.

Once a blessing is given it is done. Secondly, Noah cursing Canaan was not a direct result of Ham's

disrespectful observance. Noah's cursing of Canaan was revealed because of what was revealed to Noah about Canaan and he was angry with Ham. Noah was a prophet and God likely revealed things to Noah and prior to the incident Noah was obedient and behaved as a prophet and patriarch should. However, I speculate when Noah awoke from his wine he revealed to Ham what was going to happen to Canaan which I believe through my research that he was supposed to keep to himself. Please consider that prophet Noah had received revelation about what his descendants were going to do in the future. The revelations caused heaviness of heart upon Noah and he chose to lighten his heart with drunkenness. When Noah awoke from his wine, he acted out as a regular man might act. Instead of concealing revelation he revealed revelation.

Notice in Genesis Chapter 9 that Noah died after revealing the curses, blessings, and enlarging of his sons

and one grandson. Later in the bible Moses acted like a regular man and gave into the demands of the complaining people and because of his disobedience he was not able to enter the promise land. Henceforth, the promise land is what Canaan's curse is really about.

According to the book of Jubilees, Noah's sons divided the earth unto three sections which they were to inhabit. Consider that the ark rested upon Mt. Ararat which is in modern day Turkey. The family came down from the mountains after the flood and migrated in the modern day Middle East. Japheth and his descendants inherited the north through the Caucasus Mountains and modern day Europe. Shem and his descendants inherited modern day Middle East and Asia and Ham and his descendants inherited the south which is modern day Africa. Therefore, Canaan's inheritance

was in the continent of Africa.

The book of Jubilees 9: 14 states: And thus the sons of Noah divided unto their sons in the presence of Noah their father, and he bound them all by an oath, imprecating a curse on every one that sought to seize the portion which had not fallen (to him) by his lot. Canaan and his descendants seized a land that belonged to Shem and his descendants. That is why the bible called the promise land the land of Canaan. Noah knew that Canaan was going to wickedly take land that did not belong to him. According to the book of Jubilees Noah and his sons knew who was going to inherit each land prior to the drunken cursing episode and they all agreed upon it. Jubilees 9:15 states: And they all said, 'So be it; so be it ' for themselves and their sons forever throughout their generations till the day of judgment, on which the Lord God shall judge them with a sword

and with fire for all the unclean wickedness of their errors, wherewith they have filled the earth with

transgression and uncleanness and fornication and sin. For those of us which have read and understood the bible we know that the Canaanites were considered a wicked people full of transgressions and sin to the point the Israelites the descendants of Shem were told not to intermingle or marry them. Nevertheless, this book will discuss the wickedness of the Canaanites later in this book.

There have been several Giant skulls and skeletons discovered but again they disappear and people do not have access to research. There have been many sightings of what people claim to be the Loch Ness monster, an underwater dinosaur, or a sea serpent. These observations are generally brushed off by the public and media. Very little attention is given to anything that seems strange but might be true. The truth is we do not know what is in the deepest parts

of the ocean because we don't have that technology. Furthermore, there are mythological stories that seem unrealistic but I have to question if there might be some truthfulness in the proposed fictional stories such as one about Semiramis.

The bible does not mention a woman named Semiramis. She is said to be the mother and later the wife of Nimrod. Nimrod is the great grandson of Noah and the son of Cush. Therefore, if Semiramis was a real woman she was either a wife or concubine of Cush who is one of Ham's four sons mentioned in the bible. Upon researching the internet about Semiramis you can find various stories about her relationship to

Nimrod but I was hard pressed to find anything about her relationship to Cush. The bible clearly states that Cush is the father of Nimrod but the bible does not name the mother. The website **www.geni,com** list Quarnibil as a wife of Cush and the granddaughter of Japheth.

The Book of Jasher 7:23 states: And Cush the son of Ham, the son of Noah, took a wife in those days in his old age, and she bare a son, and they called his name Nimrod, saying, "At that time, the sons of men again began to rebel and transgress against God, and the child grew up, and his father loved him exceedingly, for he was the son of his old age." Therefore, according to the Book of Jasher Cush did have a wife and child with a woman different from Cush's other children. Henceforth, the possibility of Cush's last wife being Semiramis is a possibility.

The legend of Semiramis places her as the Queen of Babylon and also the Moon Goddess. Semiramis was also known as Ishtar and Isis. She also has different names in different cultures such as Venus, Aphrodite,

Artemis, and Diana just to name a few. If what various resources say about Semiramis is true, her

wickedness is greater than Jezebel. Semiramis is said to have a son named Tammuz who was mentioned in the bible once. She is believed to be the originator of Pagan worship that we still have today regarding Christmas on December 25th and Ishtar/Easter. I suggest that you research her yourself because she could be a chapter to herself. Nevertheless, let's speculate a little about Semiramis.

According to a Google search Semiramis' mother is a fish goddess (mermaid) named Derketo - Atargatis (Syrian goddess). Her father was supposed to be mortal. Hypothetically, speaking let's suppose that Semiramis' father died in the great deluge (Noah's Flood) but Semiramis' mother Derketo survived because she was a hybrid half human and half fish. The legend says that Derketo abandoned Semiramis at birth but then drowned herself. This scenario makes no sense if she was half fish and could live underwater. However,

I propose in my hypothesis that she knew she was going to die after child birth therefore abandoning her daughter. She had to give birth in human form and was unable to regain her fish tail and died on the beach near the water. Henceforth, sounds crazy so far...right?

Let's examine the scripture from the Book of Genesis 6:4 which states: There were giants in the earth in those days; and also after that, when the sons of God came in unto the daughters of men, and they bare children to them, the same became mighty men which were of old, men of renown. The scripture says there were giants in the earth in those days and then after that

we know that the giants died in the flood because all life of the earth and the air were destroyed in the flood.

However, the bible did not say the creatures of the sea were destroyed. If the story about Semiramis' mother being a fish goddess were true, then she could have

passed her Giant/Nephillim seed to her daughter. Therefore, if Semiramis either married or had a relationship with Cush she could pass her Giant/Nephillim seed to their son Nimrod. Nimrod would fit what was mentioned in Genesis 6:4 when it stated that they bared children unto them and the same mighty men which were of old and renown. However, instead of the male being a Giant, Nephillim, or sons of God which were fallen angels that seed would come through the female. Genesis 10:8 states: And Cush begat Nimrod: he began to be a mighty one in the earth. If Nimrod was a Nephillim after the flood that would explain how he was able to dominate the rest of the men of the earth. The bible emphasized that he was a mighty hunter before the Lord. Nimrod was likely a hunter of men and struck fear in all those around him.

If Nimrod sowed his seed and had some daughters that married the children of Canaan (such as the Philistines)

that would explain how some descendants of the Canaanites became giants. Remember, during this time the earth was of one speech and the people was not separated. Therefore, all the sons, grandsons, and great grandsons of Noah were in close proximity until God dispersed the people at the Tower of Babel. Most bible scholars will not mix scriptures with folklore which I understand because folklore is not a scholarly reference.

However, I find many situations in the bible truthful but incomplete. I cannot prove my hypothesis but under the circumstances I believe it should be considered a possibility.

There are various other theories about how giants came back but I will not go into detail about the theories. The most important thing about reading the

scriptures consist of studying and pondering the road for yourself to gain your own understanding. Insomuch,

what I have done with this book from reading for myself, studying, pondering, and applying knowledge through prayer. Just like the gospels of Matthew, Mark, Luke, and John they each tell of some of the same stories but each has different details. Likewise, you may read some of the same passages and have similar comprehension but have different perspective.

We live in the information age meaning that we have access to various amounts of information at the clock of the mouse on a computer. When I was in high school and a college undergraduate I had to research by reading various books which was time consuming and

tedious. However, upon working in my career and going back to school to earn graduate degrees and change my career the internet was available. The access to information was convenient and became fun when researching information about personal interest. In the midst of my graduate and then doctoral programs I

learned that you had to use discernment and research and could depend on scholarly articles.

Now I am free from the confines of writing a paper for school and I challenge not only books and articles that can be published by anyone but who merits what is fact or fiction. Insomuch, though I fully accept the bible to be the word of God I believe there were books intentionally left out by those who were in authority at that time to make decisions. Henceforth, now is the time to stretch our imagination in search of truth.

Chapter 5: Sexual Sins of Biblical Men

Judah and Tamar
by The Minister Artist

The bible has several passages that warn us about lust. Proverbs 6:25 states: Lust not after her beauty in thine heart; neither let her take thee with her eyelids. Many men loose themselves when an attractive woman pays them attention and may fall victim to them if they are ungodly. Proverbs 6:26 states: For by means of a whorish woman a man is brought to a piece of bread: and the adulteress will hunt for the precious life. Samson and Delilah is an example of such a woman. Delilah was commissioned to find out Samson's secret to his power to use it against him. The story baffles me because I do not understand why Samson gave into Delilah and told her the truth about his strength. I could understand it better if Samson was new to women but he was not. Samson had a lot of experience with women and he could see through Delilah. Yet there was something about Delilah that kept him coming back to her and putting himself in potentially

harm's way. I don't believe that it was just her beauty because there were many beautiful women in the world. Insomuch, I believe that she was doing something sexually that he could not get enough of something that she performed at a higher level more than a common prostitute.

Delilah could have been a witch or used witchcraft. The bible did not mention that she was a witch but it would not be a surprise if she was involved in cultic activities. Each time Samson sinned with Delilah that allowed her to gain more and more power over Samson. Eventually, she broke Samson down and he confessed the source of his strength. Samson disregarded his Godly anointing to seek selfish gratification of the flesh. I used to think Samson who was physically powerful was emotionally weak. I thought it was really dumb of Samson to keep going

back to Delilah but let alone eventually tell her the truth knowing she was trying to capture you. Nevertheless, witchcraft is no match for the power of God. However, if an anointed vessel God continually puts him in dangerous situations way eventually he could weaken and eventually give into the temptation.

King David was an anointed man of God who was blessed to serve the Lord. However, lust overcome David as he watched a woman bath from the roof of his kingdom. Second Samuel 11:2 states: And it came to pass in an evening tide, that David arose from off his bed, and walked upon the roof of the king's house:

and from the roof he saw a woman washing herself; and the woman was very beautiful to look upon. King David sent for the Bathsheba to have a sexual relationship with her and she became pregnant. If committing adultery was not bad enough David furthered his deceitfulness by trying to influence

Bathsheba's husband Uriah, the Hitite, by getting him drunk with the hope that he would sleep with his wife so he would think he was the father of the baby. However, David's efforts for Uriah to sleep with Bathsheba failed and that left David with a serious dilemma. King David became desperate and he knew that he had to do something soon before Uriah found out that his wife was pregnant by another man. Second Samuel 11:15 states: And he wrote in the letter, saying, "Set ye Uriah in the forefront of the hottest battle, and retire ye from him, that he may be smitten, and die."

King David decided to kill a man to cover his sin. Nathan the prophet confronted and convicted David about his wrong. David wept bitterly and repented of his deeds. Even though David was sorrowful he still had a price to pay which resulted in him and Bathsheba losing their first baby. God did not allow the union

between David and Bathsheba to remain and they were blessed to have another child. However, their next baby Solomon became heir to the throne over his older brothers who were born to David through other women. 2 Samuel 5:13 states: And David took him more concubines and wives out of Jerusalem, after he was come from Hebron: and there were yet sons and daughters born to David. Unfortunately, David's sins may have been the cause for trouble among his children with different mothers which included a brother and sister rape, a brother to brother murder, and one of his sons trying to overtake the throne.

David's son Solomon was once considered the wisest of all kings. During his reign he built the temple to the Lord and increased the kingdom with many riches. Solomon's fame reached across the world and it was primarily a time of peace during his reign. Solomon learned of the power of a woman and the

influence potential they have over men. 1 Kings 11:3 states: And he had seven hundred wives, princesses, and three hundred concubines: and his wives turned away his heart. The women turned the wisest person mentioned in the bible heart away from God. Solomon's heart was different than his father's heart as he aged. 1Kings 11:4 states: For it came to pass, when Solomon was old, that his wives turned away his heart

after other gods: and his heart was not perfect with the Lord his God, as was the heart of David his father. David got his heart right with God after his sin with

Bathsheba. Solomon did not get his heart back right with God because the various women turned his heart away from God. It is not known if Solomon had sex

with all of his wives or concubines but hypothetically if he decided to give each wife or concubine one day it would take him over 3 years to rotate back to the first

wife. However, that would give all the wives plenty of time to conspire against him to turn his heart away from the Most High God's will.

One of the more disturbing stories regarding sex in the bible was about Lot and his two daughters. Prior to Lot and his families escape from Sodom he was in the company of two men who were angels. Lot obviously had high regard for the angels because he was protecting them from the wicked homosexual men of Sodom who wanted to gang rape them. Lot offered the wicked men of Sodom his two daughters to leave the angels alone. Genesis 19:8 states: Behold now, I have two daughters which have not known man; let me, I pray you, bring them out unto you, and do ye to them as is good in your eyes: only unto these men do nothing; for therefore came they under the shadow of my roof. I am so glad that I have never been in a position to sacrifice a child of mine. Nevertheless, I

can't imagine any parent sacrificing a child of mine to sexual violence but even today parents have traded the sexual favors of their child to feed their addictions to various drugs.

Can you imagine how Lot's daughters must have felt when they heard their father willing to sacrifice them to protect what they perceived were two men? Fortunately, they did not have to suffer the fate because the men of Sodom did not want them and the two angels blinded the men of the town. The angels told Lot that they were going to destroy the city. Therefore, the angels inquired of who lived with Lot and instructed them to get out of town in the morning.

When Lot found out about the destruction of the city he told his wife, two daughters, and his two sons in law to get out of town. What about to mention next is one of the "things that make me say huh?"

In Genesis 9:8 Lot told the men of Sodom that his daughters have not known man. In Genesis 9:14 Lot tells his sons in law to get up and get out of Sodom but they did not believe him and did nothing. My question is, did Lot lie to the men of Sodom about their virginity or were his daughters married and still virgins. Another "thing that makes me say huh?" is where were the sons in law located when the men from Sodom were banging on Lot's door and he offered his daughters which was their wives as a sacrifice? The daughters had to be inside with Lot away from their husbands. What were both sons in law doing when they were away from their wives? Is it possible that the sons in law were similar in sexual orientation as the men who were banging on Lot's door and even though they were married they were not interested in sex with women? Unfortunately, for the sons in law they did not heed to the instructions.

Lot's wife also did not heed to the instructions. Lot and his family were instructed not to look back as the escaped the destruction of Sodom and Gomorrah. Genesis 19:26 states: But his wife looked back from behind him, and she became a pillar of salt. Her death left Lot without a wife, the two daughters without a mother and they were without husbands because they did not come and were left behind. Insomuch, all three of them had to be sad, terrified, and lonely for spousal companionship.

Lot and his daughters thought they were the last remaining people on earth. The older daughter spoke to the younger daughter about having sex with their father to get pregnant and preserve human kind. Genesis 19:32 states: Come, let us make our father drink wine, and we will lie with him, that we may preserve seed of our father. Genesis 19:33 states: And they made their

father drink wine that night: and the firstborn went in, and lay with her father; and he perceived not when she lay down, nor when she arose. My next "things that make you say huh?" consist of how did the daughters being virgins know how to get their father drunk enough to have sex with him and how did they know they know what to do. Furthermore, the bible states that Lot did not know when they laid down with him and when they arose. Please forgive me for being graphic in my next statements/questions I will soften it up as much as I can. How did the daughters make their father's nature rise in such a drunken state and how did they know when he was going to reach the happy point to put his seed into them? I had experienced as a young man what they call a wet dream meaning that you can be sleep, have your nature rise, and reach a happy point. Unfortunately, today women and men have been

penetrated when passed out while being intoxicated. It is not common for the man to receive when passed out. Nevertheless, that is what happed with Lot and his daughters. The bible tells us that both daughters became pregnant from their father. Genesis 19:37 & 38 tells us that the offspring of the conceptions become the Moabites and the Ammonites who were considered wicked people in the bible. However, there was one exception regarding wickedness which is the righteousness of the Moabites Ruth.

The bible tells of other sexual stories such as the rape of Dinah the daughter of Jacob/Israel and Tamar the daughter of King David by her brother. There are love stories such as The Song of Solomon with the Queen of Sheba. There are many instances of a man knowing (knew) his wife which means have sex then having children. A couple other sexual references

include take (took), went into a woman. The Book of Leviticus in the King James Version will use the term uncover (have sex) nakedness (person having sex with) in regarding forbidden sexual relations. Henceforth, there are many references to sex in the bible and endless genealogies about who begat who.

One curious story in the bible was in regards to Judah the son of Jacob/Israel. Judah apparently had an attraction for Canaanite women which Abraham and Isaac warned their children not to marry. Abraham said to his servant he sent to find a wife for Isaac in Genesis 24:3 And I will make thee swear by the Lord, the God of heaven, and the God of the earth, that thou shalt not take a wife unto my son of the daughters of the Canaanites, among whom I dwell:. Isaac the son of Abraham also gave his son Jacob the same direction to not to marry a Canaanite a woman before blessing him. By this time Jacob's brother Esau had married two

Canaanite women. Isaac stated in Genesis 28:1 And Isaac called Jacob, and blessed him, and charged him, and said unto him, "Thou shalt not take a wife of the daughters of Canaan." The Canaanites were known to be sinful and disrespectful to the ways of the Lord. Nevertheless, in Genesis 38:2 And Judah saw there a daughter of a certain Canaanite, whose name was Shuah; and he took her, and went in unto her.

Judah's Canaanite wife bore him a son named Er who grew to be wicked before the Lord. She would bare two more sons to Judah. Judah found a wife for his son Er by the name of Tamar who was likely a Canaanite woman. Er the son of Judah and husband of Tamar was slain because of his wickedness and he did not have a son. The custom of that time consisted of the next brother taking his dead brothers wife and have a child through her on his brother's behalf. Onan was the brother next in line and he was resentful of the custom. Genesis 38:9 states: And Onan knew that the seed should not be his; and it came to pass, when he went in unto his brother's wife, that he spilled it on the ground, lest that he should give seed to his brother. Onan spilling his seed on the ground displeased the Lord and he was slain. This left one last brother whose name was Shelah but he was not an adult. Therefore, Judah told Tamar to remain a widow until his last son was grown and to go back to her father's house until it was time.

Tamar did as Judah instructed but he never sent for her after Shelah was grown. During that time Judah's wife died and was sad and lonely and looked to be comforted. Judah planned to go to the location of Timnath and be with his friend Hurah the Adullamite

and Tamar heard of Judah's plans. Genesis 38:14: states: And she put her widow's garments off from her,

and covered her with a vail, and wrapped herself, and

sat in an open place, which is by the way to Timnath; for she saw that Shelah was grown, and she was not given unto him to wife. Judah seen Tamar but he did not know who she was and thought she was a prostitute because of how she was dressed. Judah asked to have sex with her and he made a pledge with her that included giving Tamar his signet, bracelets, and staff. They had sex and she did become pregnant but she returned to her widow clothes. When Judah returned home he sent his pledge. When his servant returned there was not a harlot/prostitute to be found. Judah became stressed about not keeping his pledge but later he received information about Tamar his daughter in law. Genesis 38:24 states: And it came to pass about three months after, that it was told Judah, saying, Tamar thy daughter in law hath played the harlot;

and also, behold, she is with child by whoredom. And Judah said, "Bring her forth, and let her be burnt." Hypocritically, Judah was going to pass judgment upon Tamar when he knowingly sought the services of a prostitute.

Tamar's wisdom saved her life when she presented the signet, bracelets, and staff she received from the father of her child. Judah was immediately shamed and stated that she was more righteous than his self because he purposely withheld his son from her. Ironically, they never had sex again but Tamar would bare Judah twin sons I which through his son Pharez was the lineage of the Messiah Jesus Christ.

Chapter 6: Destruction of the Family

Genesis Chapter 16 Sarah, Abraham and Hagar by The Minister Artist

God places high value on the family unit and Satan places high value on destroying the family unit. In the Book of Genesis alone brothers fought against and hated each other. Cain killed his brother Abel. Esau wanted to kill his brother Jacob. Jacob's sons hated his son Joseph through his favorite wife Rachel and they left him for dead before they decided to sell him into slavery. They took the deception a step further and lied to their father letting him believe he was dead. Jacob conspired with his mother Rebecca to deceive Isaac into giving Jacob the blessing instead of Esau. Jacob was deceived by his uncle Laban into marrying Leah instead of Rachel and had to commit to seven more years of working for him to marry Rachel. Insomuch, women drama and baby mama drama has been around for a long time.

Jacob never hid that Rachel was his favorite wife

that had to make Leah feel unloved and unwanted. It

was through obligation that Jacob honored husbandly duties with her. Through obligation Leah was fertile and gave Jacob sons while Rachel was temporarily barren which created envy of Rachel towards her sister Leah. The situation became so competitive and silly that when the sisters were not producing children they gave their maids as concubines to Jacob to produce children through them. Henceforth, when it was over there were 12 sons produced by four different women.

Abraham and Sarah had a situation with children where she brought in her maid Hagar to give her husband an heir. Problems between Sarah and Hagar arouse when Hagar flaunted her pregnancy. Sarah in her humanly state did not understand that God was capable of opening her womb to fulfill the promise that she would bare Abraham a son. Multiple women and wives to men had never really worked and it was not God's plan. God created a woman for a man and a husband for a wife. King David's peace within his kingdom was changed after he committed adultery with Bathsheba. Their first born son died as part of a consequence for the sin. Their son Solomon who was once the wisest of all kings and faithful to the Lord had his heart turned away from God because of the multitude and wickedness of his wives and concubines. In modern times there are and have been men with multiple wives. The wives usually have little or no voicing of their opinions because the men are dominant and usually egotistical. Ironically, today we have many female heads of the household and men and women who refuse to marry but have children out of wedlock which has become common place in some communities.

The destruction of the family is one of Satan's main goals to undermine God. The strength of

families come from God when families make God a priority in their lives. However, when God is not a priority in a family's lives you will find dysfunction and chaos. Insomuch before I use biblical examples I must begin this chapter with my personal dysfunction.

I am somewhat ashamed to admit that when I began writing this book, things were on the upswing between me and my wife. After beginning to write this book, things began to change and new and old challenges arose. The word divorce was discussed a few times which was devastating to me. However, the truth is I haven't been the best husband or the best father to my children. To make matters worse I became dull and predictable stuck in my old habits. However, one habit I called on the grace of God through His Son Jesus pornography.

I became addicted to pornography subtly by

sneaking and looking at dirty magazines. When I turned 18, I was able to buy my own dirty magazines. When I was growing up my parents had cable television including the paid channels (not the Playboy Channel) and I would stay up late to watch sexually charged R-rated (soft porn) movies. I had a girlfriend in college who had access to one of her family member's X-rated video collection and we would watch them together. After that point I would watch them on my own and by myself. After graduation from college and living on my own I would often rent X-rated videos and have private

date nights with myself if I did not have female company or did not want to be bothered. I did not realize the spiritual damage I was causing myself. The activities I was indulging in were legal and accepted by mainstream society. However, I knew that something was not right about it because I was living a double life because I did not disclose my activities to family members or friends. Nevertheless, I continued with my habits even up until meeting my future wife.

My future wife was different from my other girlfriends. She was the first person I felt comfortable discussing the bible with. She was not a drinker or a partier like I was at that time. She grounded me and made me feel safe to discuss things that I never shared with anyone. However, I never discussed in detail or the depth of my secret addiction. I still did not think too much over my addiction and did not think that it would be a hindrance in the marriage. Oddly, enough during the wedding ceremony the bishop quoted from the bible as he was reading our vows and stated: Matthew 5:28 But I say unto you, "That whosoever looketh on a woman to lust after her hath committed adultery with her already in his heart." I said to myself what are you saying and how did you know. I always thought you could look and not touch and be safe. I was spiritually shaken at my wedding because I made up my mind that I would not physically have sex with anyone besides my wife but I thought I thought I could have my dreams about women I found attractive. However, the bible says that if I have my day dreams I am guilty of adultery.

Adultery is one tool that Satan uses to destroy the family. It is not just the husbands, but many wives are guilty of adultery, whether it's physical, mental, or emotional. Financial issues are another tool Satan uses to destroy the family. In a typical wedding ceremony, you hear the words "for better or worse", "richer or poorer", and "in sickness or health" but few want to commit to the alternatives (poorer, worse, or sickness). There are so many divorces that take place because people are either too vain or emotionally fragile to deal

with the alternatives. People call it irreconcilable

differences and get a divorce or an annulment. Christians get divorced at a similar rate as the world which is sad to me because having Christ in your marriage should make a greater difference. Nevertheless, people are growing more selfish and unwilling to sacrifice for the sake of another.

Selfishness is the main cause for problems in

a marriage. I should know because my wife has accused me of being selfish many times in our marriage and she was right. My selfishness made it difficult for me to be motivated to do anything that I would not benefit from. My wife is a wonderfully unique woman with a heart of gold. Her willingness to give and share often conflicted with my stinginess. Her willingness to sacrifice her time often conflicted with my desire for me time. I don't know how she put up with me as I have matured spiritually. Fortunately, for us we have both been angry with one another at times and embarrassingly I have failed my wife with broken promises I can say that we have never resulted to violence or verbal abuse. Unfortunately, some couples cannot make the claim of no violence, verbal abuse, or physical adultery.

On a very personal note, I nearly lost my marriage. My wife was sick of me and my selfishness. I was consumed with gratifying my flesh. Not just sexually but with food and electronic stimulation. Addiction to pornography robs a marriage of natural love and affection because pornography is designed to make a person seek unrealistic fantasies. The more you view pornography the less in touch with reality and more perverse you become. I was not a good husband or father during the peak of my addiction. I created some selfish habits that were difficult to overcome. Unfortunately, I did not make spending quality time

with my family a priority and made them feel alienated

and uncared about. The pain that I caused them occurred over some years and was not easily repaired. Thankfully, we have a loving Savior and His grace prevailed and my family was saved when I finally began to face the truth about myself.

There are too many problems to name when it comes to marriage or family issues. It must be stated even though Satan gets the blame for planning the destruction of the family Satan cannot do it without willing participants who chose to engage in certain actions and behaviors. Individuals open the door be entertaining wicked thoughts that they act upon and open a gateway for satanic demons to enter into them. Satanic activity is always present in our lives through the media, agents, and unhappy people who do not wish others well. Christians are spiritually strong enough to overcome satanic devices of enticement, manipulation and fear. However, when Christians are emotionally drained or physically exhausted they may temporarily give into to the weaknesses of the flesh. Satan knows this so he uses his angels, demons and agents (people) to distract and refocus our attention away from God's purposes for our lives. Insomuch, there are non-Christian organizations that have goals to destroy the family unit.

According to an article in Seven James Word Press drug use, pornography, sexual revolutions, feminism, homosexuality, and polygamy are aspects that will destroy family life that the human race was built upon. The same article describes unemployment and cultural rebellion will lead to a devastated workforce that will turn to drugs and alcohol and become dependent on the state (welfare) to take care of them. The article states that children will be introduced to nonpolitical rebellion and ungodly behaviors will be introduced by celebrities that will assist in breaking down the family unit. Popular media will be used to promote propaganda through subliminal prompts in cartoons, popular media, and celebrity opinion knowing that these tactics can heavily influence children into wrong thinking. Education of children is also under attack to dumb down generations by undermining the curriculum and over estimating student achievement. Furthermore, the article in Seven James Press talked about many other issues pertaining to the goals of a certain secret society.

In this day and age, it cannot be easy to be a child. Years ago everybody knew and understood their role in the family. The man was supposed to work and provide for the family, the woman nurtured the children and took care of home; the children were respectful of their parents and adults. Some women worked outside o help their husbands provide for the needs of the home and men also supported and helped with needs of the home and primarily did all of the outside chores. I am not saying that women cannot be the bread winner or men should be shamed if they work in the home. I am saying that it is confusion when mommy and daddy are the same sex. I am saying that is not God's best plan if a man is able body to work but chooses not to. I am saying it is not pleasing to God when a woman despises motherhood and mistreats her children. Baby momma's and baby daddy's is not part of God's plan. Marriage is undervalued and almost despised by the youth. The old saying goes, "Why but the cow when you can get the milk for free?" The greatest deception in this category is free love. We should love and accept everybody for who they are and what they are doing. While it is true

that we are commanded to love our neighbors as ourselves we are not commanded to accept behavior

contrary to the word of God. Insomuch, the rapper/ actor Tupac Shakur once said in one of his songs paraphrasing from the bible says "don't judge me" needs to be expounded upon.

At this day and age most of us have someone in our family who has declared that they are gay. If you don't have someone in your family, you probably have a friend or know someone that you went to school with that lives a homosexual lifestyle. If you have real love or concern for a person you cannot stop loving them because of their actions especially if it does not alter what you do and how you live. God does love everyone. However, God speaks against all sexual sin and behavior. Satan and his workers put thoughts in our heads all day. We have to have enough discernment to understand that all thoughts our not our thoughts. We have the ability to reject thoughts. I have heard people say that they were born gay or they knew they were gay at a young age. I believe people only have a limited amount of control to what they are attracted too but they do have some control. We have to manage which thoughts we entertain and which thoughts we rebuke. God's plan for us was for man and woman to be fruitful and to multiply. Therefore, God did not create homosexuality in heaven or anywhere else.

The bible tells us more than once that God is not a respecter of persons. Therefore, we should not be either. No person on earth has the right to look down on another person nor should people make other people more valuable than others because they have something that we consider important (money, fame, status, similar values, etc.). When God commanded us to "love our neighbor as ourselves" that included everybody regardless of their religious beliefs, socio-economic status, sexual orientation, gender, skin color,

ethnicity, or age. God created us with a purpose however when most of us come to earth we think that we are our own. Satan drills into our heads that the body we have is ours and we can do what we want. Many people think that worship of Satan is murder, sex, rape, and torture. Although, that is part of the elite marriage is between and man and a woman Satan says marry whom you like. God says sex is for married spouses only Satan says have sex with who you like. God says to honor your mother and father Satan says you only honor those you think are worthy and you can be disrespectful if they deserve it. God says that He loves humility and hates pride Satan says be proud of your defiance. God loves families with the husband, mother, and children. Satan hates the family structure and seeks to destroy it. Essentially, whatever the bible

says that God wants us to do, Satan will have you do

the opposite.

Satan knows that he cannot overcome strong Christian families when the man is under the authority of Jesus Christ and compliant to God's words. Female heads of the household who are strong believers will also be strong against Satan as well as single people who are strong in faith. Husband (man), wife (woman), and children who are a house that serves the Lord. Satan sends prompts to disrupt the home by any means necessary. Satan knows if he can make the family unit selfish by means of fear, distrust, confusion, and distracting the home from God that he can create chaos.

Technology and media has taken over many households already. Many individual families are busy doing their own thing and do not sit at the dinner table to eat a meal together or if they do they are checking their smart phones. You can find people off task in church as well. Yes, some people are using their phones to pull up scriptures but some are doing who knows what at church. The church family use to be the backbone of the community. Unfortunately, with many sex and money scandals of preachers that has been posted in the media the trust and reverence of pastors has declined in the public eye. Also with so called prosperity preachers many have the public perception that pastors only want your money so they can live a luxurious life style. I personally believe that most preachers start off with the intent to serve God and deliver his word. However, pastors are human and are capable of getting caught up in the flesh like anyone else. Yet I still believe most preachers heard the call to serve the Lord to lead people and families to the Lord. Nevertheless, without naming men of God who have fallen I will summarize by saying a lot of damage has been done by them that deter many men to going to church and coming under authority of church leadership.

Many men who do not value church do not seek Christ as their head and by doing so allow openings for the house to be out of order. There are many women who desire their husbands to be the "head of the household" not by the flesh but by the leadership of the spirit. Nevertheless, there are many good men in the world and many good husbands and fathers who get overlooked by the world. They are overlooked because they are not flashy or braggadocios but are humble servants of the Lord. It is sad to me when there are good single men available but some single women are looking for a fairy tale romance and knight in shining armor. Likewise, when men only look at a woman's physical attributes or the opposite and use her to live

off of her substance. Worldly, fleshly men may have

money, status, and looks but lack a relationship with God. Mark 8:36 states: For what shall it profit a man, if he shall gain the whole world, and lose his own soul?

The lack of family values is a direct result of selfishness and fulfilling the flesh. We live in a society that is driven by money, notoriety, and self-gratification. Many people see children as a burden instead of a blessing. If there is an unwanted pregnancy a woman can decide on her own without the consent of the man to have the child aborted. They are unknowingly sacrificing their child to the modern day Baal called Planned Parenthood. Families today practice and celebrate many things that are rooted in paganism which is a different discussion. Deuteronomy 23:17 states: There shall be no whore of the daughters of

Israel, nor a sodomite of the sons of Israel. Unfortunately, this can and will happen without God's

family unit.

Technology has its role in the declining values of the family. Family members are often attached to their cell phones even at the dinner table. The dinner table used to have a lot of value in many families where they could talk and share what is taking place in their daily lives. Computer games, video games, and other electronic devices have many families eating meals in different locations or at different times. Technology itself can do nothing to destroy the family unit but the individuals within the family unit can make decisions that may cause distance between family members because of their usage of technology. Henceforth, technology itself is merely a tool that can be used by individuals nut I have seen people's usage of technology cause problems in relationships.

The family relationships are very important. I should

know because I have been guilty of making excuses and

causing hurt feelings within my family unit. Even though I considered myself a Christian I was not always putting God as the head of my household. I often placed my job as the head of my household followed by my selfish desires to relax or quality me time as my daily priorities. It was a costly error.

Chapter 7: The Skin I am In

Human Body & Spirit Body
by The Minister Artist

First and foremost, none of us could control how much melanin we were born with. We received our physical attributes from our earthly parents and our spiritual being from our Heavenly Father. The truth is that we are all different shades of brown. I agree with Ken Ham's research but I believed we are all shades of brown prior to learning about his research on genetics. Again so called black people and so called white people do not exist. Everyone on the planet Earth is either a dark, light, or mid-tone shade of brown. If people were truly either black or white when they interbreed their children would be born some variation of gray. The evidence shows that when so called black people interbreed with so called white people their off spring is usually

a middle tone of brown between both parents. In the early 20th century United States people were considered white or colored. If a white person interbred with a colored person, the child was considered

colored. Insomuch, people during that time period put a great deal of emphasis on race.

The races of people were created by man. God created people and within the people God created were different tribes or families of people. One of my favorite research tools is Bible Gateway because I can quickly look up scriptures. I researched the word "race" in Bible Gateway in multiple versions. The King James Version mentioned race four times but each time was referring to a contest of running. The older bible versions refer to race as a contest of running. However, newer bible versions including The New King James Version make a reference or references to race as a group of people, human race, or mixed race. Henceforth, the question is why the newer bible version introduced the context of race regarding people and the

older bible versions only referred to race as a contest of

running. I propose the possible conspiracy or hidden agenda to justify the ideology of racial superiority. The bible has been manipulated to confirm the belief of one human race being superior to another human race. I propose the possible conspiracy or hidden agenda to justify the ideology of racial superiority. The bible has been manipulated to confirm the belief of one human race being superior to another human race.

The real deal is if we do not choose Jesus Christ/ Yeshua or whichever name you call the Messiah you will not be chosen. Matthew 22:14, For many are called but few are chosen. Regardless, of our so called race we need a savior. Matthew 7:14 states: Because strait is the gate, and narrow is the way, which leadeth unto life, and few there be that find it. Therefore, our preachers need to stop only teaching the broad way to eternal life. There are things that the Body of Christ has to stop tolerating and participating in that is contrary to the

word of God. We act like we are in a time of peace but our spiritual lives are on the line daily. We are in a spiritual war and we are not building our spiritual strength by focusing on the color of our flesh. Nevertheless, with that said most of us have been duped into believing the image of Jesus with blue eyes and long blondish or brown hair as being how Messiah looked when he walked the earth.

If you casually study art, history, geography, genetics, and the bible to any degree you will have to notice that some of the things that we have been taught do not add up. The chances of Jesus walking the earth in the so called Middle East as a so called white man with blue eyes and long blondish or brown hair is unlikely based upon geography and genetics. I left out history because that may be His Story whoever he may be. I left out art because that can be subjective to either the artist or who is financing the work of art. During the Renaissance Period the Catholic Church commissioned Leonardo Da Vinci, Michelangelo and others to create artwork to their liking even at the dismay of the artist. Many people were illiterate in those days so the artwork of the time was their teacher along with the words of priests, bishops, and the Popes. The images created by artists were engraved in the minds of the people of that time as being the truth. Today the media has the greatest effect on the people. I have engraved in my mind that Moses looking like Charlton Heston who was a great actor. However, Moses likely did not look like him. Henceforth, who did Jesus and Moses look like becomes the question.

The truth is that nobody living today was alive during those times. Therefore, we cannot conclude how Jesus or Moses looked conclusively. Nevertheless, the images engraved in people's minds can create a feeling of superiority or inferiority. Archeology, architecture, ancient artwork, history, and the bible itself contradict the images that we received of biblical figures as children and adults through the media. Jesus and Moses both spent time in Egypt so let's evaluate Egypt first. The pyramids have artwork inside of them that depict primarily people with brown hues. Multiple sculptures including the Sphinx have the nose defaced and some have the lips defaced as well. It is believed that the sculptures had features that depicted features of people who were brown to dark brown such as a wider nose and thicker lips. For those of you who may doubt what I stated do a simple Google search of Egyptian cave art or Egyptian defaced sculptures and come to your own conclusion. However, consider that both Moses and Jesus were hidden in Egypt as babies to spare their

lives. Therefore, they must have looked like the people

who were living there at the time.

An angel of God told Joseph to take Mary and baby Jesus to Egypt to hide from King Herod. King Herod was aware of the prophecy of a Messiah being born went on to kill all male babies of age 3 years and under. Similarly, Pharaoh of Egypt was aware of a prophecy of a Messiah being born and he killed the Hebrew male babies 3 years and younger. Moses was raised as an Egyptian and believed by all to be Egyptian until his true identity was revealed. He decided to follow his true heritage and left the house of Egypt. In Exodus 4:6: And the Lord said furthermore unto him, Put now thine hand into thy bosom. And he put his hand into his bosom: and when he took it out, behold, his hand was leprous as snow. We have been taught that leprosy in the bible means diseased and unclean. Exodus 4:7: states, And he said, "Put thine hand into thy bosom again." And he put his hand into his bosom again; and

plucked it out of his bosom, and, behold, it was turned again as his other flesh. However, the bible talks about unclean and clean leprosy. The Book of Leviticus Chapter 13 talks about different forms of leprosy. Freckles, balding heads, and white skin are considered clean forms of leprosy. Leviticus 13:12 & 13: And if a leprosy break out abroad in the skin, and the leprosy cover all the skin of him that hath the plague from his head even to his foot, wheresoever the priest looketh; Then the priest shall consider: and, behold, if the leprosy have covered all his flesh, he shall pronounce him clean that hath the plague: it is all turned white: he is clean. Henceforth, in today's world if a person skin turns white it is called vitiligo.

Many people have vitiligo today in blotches but some have turned all white. Michael Jackson is the most famous person whose skin changed from vitiligo. It is very possible that Moses sister Miriam suffered from blotched vitiligo when she and their brother Aaron were talking about Moses when he married an Ethiopian woman. Numbers 12:10 And the cloud departed from off the tabernacle; and, behold, Miriam became leprous, white as snow: and Aaron looked upon Miriam, and, behold, she was leprous. We know that Miriam was not turned completely white because of Numbers 12:12 which states: Let her not be as one dead, of whom the flesh is half consumed when he cometh out of his mother's womb. We could also assume that Miriam was not all turned white according to the description of clean mentioned in Leviticus 13: 12 &13. We must also consider that Miriam's leprosy could have been like the traditional belief of leprosy being a flesh consuming disease. However, I find it interesting that Aaron pleaded for her and asked that she not be like a still born infant. Her skin was shocking

to Aaron. Nevertheless, we must consider that Aaron did not say that her skin was half consumed he asked that it not be like one who was dead.

The truth is whether we are classified as black or white there is some shame associated with our ancestors. My research leads me to believe that Noah was the first human with so called white skin. Therefore, the people prior to Noah were full of melanin. So called black people were the first so called rulers of the world. Nimrod the son of Cush the son of Ham was known as the first great ruler in the world. The problem was he was a very wicked man who did not fear or respect God. Most of the pagan worship that still exists in the world today comes from Nimrod and his wife. The line of Shem the son of Noah was also full of melanin who, also are the descendants who chose Barabbas over Jesus which lead to the crucifixion of our Lord and Savior. The lineage of Judah through Abraham, Isaac, Jacob/Israel, and Shem were forced out of Jerusalem in 70 AD and dispersed to the four corners of the earth. The Curses of Deuteronomy 68 were placed upon this people for their failure to obey and honor the Most High God. They are guilty of a variety of wickedness too many to name. Insomuch, there are good achievements as well which are often left out of the history books.

The history books are filled with the achievements of those who lack melanin. Those who lack melanin often leave out of the history books the bullying, murdering, lying, stealing, abusing, violations, and oppressive behaviors. Their wickedness is substantial and barbaric growing to epic proportions of hypocrisy. Nevertheless, there are many great and true accomplishments by people who lack melanin because all history is not his story.

> There were some people years ago who decided to use the bible to justify slavery of people who are full of melanin. They used Genesis Chapter 9 when Noah cursed Ham's son Canaan as a servant of servants as justification scripture. Most biblical scholars agree that Ham's line populated Africa where people full of melanin reside. The misuse of this scripture created a feeling of superiority for some and inferiority for others. Some of the people who had the feeling of superiority called Noah's curse the "Curse of Ham" when the bible clearly states that Ham's son Canaan was cursed. The superiority mentality fails to mention that

Ham with his two brothers and father were all blessed by God and Noah could not curse what God already blessed. Furthermore, Ham had three other sons and they were not cursed.

Therefore, it was unrealistic to assume that all people full of melanin were under a curse.

To make matters worse I have read about awful theories some men in the past created to demonize Ham. I have read that Ham was cursed because he sodomized Noah. I have read that Ham was cursed because he castrated Noah because he did not want his inheritance split more ways. I have read that Ham was cursed because he had sex or raped his mother. . I do not claim Ham to be a saint but I do not believe these stories to justify slavery of people full of melanin. I have also read that Ham stole and hid the garments of Adam and Eve from his father. There is more potential truth in that narrative.

The Book of Jasher and The Legend of The Jews, both tell the story of Ham stealing the garments wore by Adam and Eve from Noah. However, I have a difficult time believing that a son with two older

brothers and a living father would physically violate either one of his parents. I stated and shared my belief that Ham watched his parents have drunken sex and fall asleep and Ham went and told his brothers what he saw. When Shem and Japheth walked backwards to cover the nakedness of Noah that would have been a perfect opportunity for Ham to steal the garments of Adam and Eve from his father and hide them somewhere they could not be found. In the King James Version in Genesis Chapter 9 and Leviticus Chapter 18 are the bases for my beliefs as stated in a previous chapter. Henceforth, skin color is not a determinate of who and should not be in slavery.

The Legend of the Jews claims that Ham the son of Noah, the raven, and a breed of dog broke a law while they were on the ark during the flood. The Legend also states: After the sacrifice was completed, God blessed

Noah and his sons. He made them to be rulers of the world as Adam had been, and He gave them a command, saying, "Be fruitful and multiply upon the earth," for during their sojourn in the ark, the two sexes, of men and animals alike, had lived apart from each other, because while a public calamity rages continence is becoming even to those who are left unscathed. This law was designed for humans and animals not to have sex while they were on the ark. The Legend of the Jews further stated in the next two sentences: This law of conduct had been violated by none in the ark except by Ham, by the dog, and by the raven. They all received a punishment. Ham's was that his descendants were men of dark-hued skin. I found this to be interesting because this would make Ham a darker brown than his brothers. All people are shades of brown whether it is light, midrange, or dark brown. However, even if this is true it does not justify slavery

of dark hued races nor was it the curse that Noah placed upon his grandson Canaan in Genesis Chapter 9.

Regardless of what the color of our skin is the most important thing is that our spirit comes from God. When we die regardless of our skin color it will turn to dust. Ecclesiastes 12:7 states: Then shall the dust return to the earth as it was: and the spirit shall return unto God who gave it. When you think about it why do people spend so much time focused on skin color? Good and bad behavior comes in all shades and sizes. Ecclesiastes 3:21-22 states: All go unto one place; all are of the dust, and all turn to dust again. Who knoweth the spirit of man that goethupward, and the spirit of the beast that goeth downward to the earth? God looks at our hearts not our skin color. Whether we are a Jew or a Gentile we are only saved when we accept Jesus

Christ as our Lord and Savior and put our faith and

trust in him. There are many people who believe they have a ticket to heaven because they are a chosen people. Some people believe their race is superior and they are more privileged in heaven. Men argue about who will and won't go to heaven. Titus 3:9 states: But avoid foolish questions, and genealogies, and contentions, and strivings about the law; for they are unprofitable and vain. Therefore, we know how to act.

Chapter 8: Compromised Christianity

Fallen to Hades
by The Minister Artist

My wife and I planned to take a year off from our home church to visit other churches while she was researching religiosity for her dissertation. We attended various churches of multiple denominations in the area that we lived in. We really enjoyed seeing the different churches and how similar and different they were to each other. Occasionally, we may come across a church that we would not go back to but that was balanced by churches we would go back to. Most churches were friendly, welcoming, and inviting. We witness some good messages, inspiring messages, and boring messages. I was not too critical of the churches because we were only getting a snapshot of each church. Nevertheless, we still made decisions whether we wanted to revisit or not based upon a snapshot of an individual church.

People make snap shots of churches and so-called

religious people all the time. Many times it is not the

preacher that turns people away from church it is the members inside of the church. I have experienced two types of church members that have turned me off to their church. Churches members who are arrogant and act as if they are above you or people who think that only their church is right and all other churches are wrong. I don't have a problem with people feeling that their church is great because they should but it is hard to deal with people who are churchy on Sunday and worldly the rest of the week. Henceforth, I should know I because I was churchy on some Sundays and worldly the rest of the days.

Most people I knew grew up in compromised Christianity at least I know that I did. I did not think twice about going to church on Sunday and drinking

beer that afternoon watching a football game. When I began my quest to read the bible and get to know the

Lord I was in the midst of fornication, drunkenness, and idolatry. Do not get me wrong because people who seek to embrace Christianity must start where you are and the grace of God is sufficient for all of our needs. However, what I am really talking about is picking and choosing what we want from the bible to make it fit us instead of changing ourselves to fit the bible.

I remember early in my self-engaged Christ walk I was fornicating and drinking. I was addicted to gratifying the flesh. However, my spirit thirsted for biblical knowledge. I had a couple of bibles and a dictionary. I read the bible for hours while I would look up the words in the bible that I did not understand. This was back in the day before the internet. I purchased bible cassettes to listen to and various books about religion. I would play the tapes at night while I went to sleep hoping that the word would get into my subconscious. I believe that it did even though I drank

every night but not to point of being drunk. I used to ignorantly manipulate the bible to fit my behavior. Ephesians 5:18 states: And be not drunk with wine, wherein is excess; but be filled with the Spirit; That was my excuse that I was able to drink as long as I did not get drunk. I was a professional drinker at that time and I knew my limits and had experienced being drunk so I knew how far I could go. Insomuch, I was a functional alcoholic who could keep a job, show flashes of excellence but never excelled. However, regarding Ephesians 5:18 when I misused the line drunk not in excess but I ignored the part about being filled with the spirit.

On November 7, 1991 Magic Johnson announced that he tested positive for the H.I.V. virus which leads to A.I.D.S. This shocked the world. His announcement shook me up and woke me up to the

fact that if a famous celebrity basketball player can get H.I.V. then I could too from having unprotected sex. This made me do some soul searching and intensified my search for truth and knowledge about biblical and spiritual matters. It also let me know that it was not safe or cool to go around trying to have sex with as many women as possible. I became convicted about my promiscuity but I did not stop my behavior I just become more cautious and selective. I started to feel guilty about my weakness to sin but I did not have the spiritual wisdom to ask God for help. I thought that I had to change on my own to find favor with God. Henceforth, I failed many times in my attempts to overcome my fleshly desires which lead me to live a guilt ridden life.

Nobody wants to feel like a failure or think they are a bad person. What many people do including me is

make excuses or compromises. I was a master of

making excuses and I could find many ways to shift blame or make things not my fault. I did not realize at the time that those excuses were trumped up lies to make me not feel guilty. Making excuses is something immature or baby Christians do to cope with mistakes, failures, or hide thing they do not want publicized. However, compromising is a little more detrimental because it involves altering the word of God to make it justify a person's life style.

I am not speaking about coming to a compromise with and individual such as your spouse, children, friend, etc. to work problems out. I am speaking about deliberately going against what the bible says not to do. I am speaking about ignoring or altering the word of God for selfish gain. Individuals may compromise their beliefs because they are afraid of offending someone, losing someone, or missing out

on personal gain such as money, power, or lust. Team sports in the past of set double standard compromises for star athletes compared to other team members in order to keep the star player happy while the other players have to conform to expectations. An organization such as a church may compromise in order to have a larger congregation and receive more revenue

from tithes and offerings. Henceforth, let's examine the church and compromised Christianity.

Compromised Christianity is not new and most people of have experienced it or grew up in it. I am not writing this to belittle people because I would have to belittle myself. My goal is to create awareness so we are not hoodwinked or bamboozled anymore. Nevertheless, the next things I will write will offend some people. The bible says that man lying with man like a woman is an abomination. Homosexuality is

our reality in the world we live in but, the House of

God is not supposed to be of this world. I'm not talking about someone repenting from homosexual activity but those who are actively engaged. Therefore, churches that either condone or ignore behaviors such as homosexuality, adultery, and fornication are churches of the world and not churches of God.

Churches of the world may often give powerful sermons and inspiring messages. There has been an attack on what has been called the prosperity gospel which emphasizes health, wealth, and positive thinking. There is absolutely nothing wrong with preaching uplifting and positive messages. However, if you do that you are only preaching a small portion of the bible. Uplifting messages will exhort the people and will not offend anyone nor will it convict anyone. Second Timothy 4:2 states: Preach the word; be instant in

season, out of season; reprove, rebuke, exhort with all

long suffering and doctrine. Therefore, preachers should exhort but they also must be timely with the word and they may offend sometimes by rebuking and reproving. The bible accurately prophesied that the time would come when people would not be interested in what is written in the bible. Second Timothy 4:3 & 4 states: For the time will come when they will not endure sound doctrine; but after their own lusts shall they heap to themselves teachers, having itching ears; And they shall turn away their ears from the truth, and shall be turned unto fables.

Many people accept Darwin's 1859 "Theory of Evolution" and some people accept Lemaitre 1927 "Big Bang Theory" instead of believing the Holy Bible. Some people today accuse the bible as being a book of fables. Instead of Darwin giving God credit for creating the universe he proposed natural selection and how organisms change over time as a result of behavioral

and physical traits. An example would be a man developed over time beginning as an ape who learned to walk upright. Lemaitre also chose not to give God credit and taught about an expanding universe that began over 13 billion years ago. Many highly earthly intelligent people have bought into world origins instead of the bible. I will not go into the details of the "Theory of Evolution" or "The Big Bang

Theory" because for me a bible believer these are some of the fables that the bible prophesied about that people will believe. Insomuch, biblical prophecies are showing evidence of accuracy while the so called great theories are still selective opinions by those who reject the bible.

Those of us who believe in the bible must accept that no one is perfect or possess all the truths. We have to be forgiving because we want to be forgiven for our mistakes. However, those of us who are hungry for the

truth and desire to please God and accept His Son Jesus Christ as Lord and Savior must love or learn to love everyone. We are allowed to judge behavior against what the bible says is right and wrong but we are not allowed to condemn people. Preachers of God will preach the word; be instant in season, out of season; reprove, rebuke, exhort with all long suffering and doctrine. Insomuch, preachers of the world will exhort mostly and only brush over anything negative not to offend. If you are able to discern you can get a good motivational message but you will not be challenged to dig deep into yourself and ask the Lord for the grace to help you. Unfortunately, the greatest problem with Compromised Christianity is the effect the behaviors of Christians have on non-believers.

Christians should be peculiar to the world but many look and act just like the world. Many Christians are not modest in their dress, speech, entertainment, or

consumption of goods. We should be following the example of Christ. Titus 2:14 refers to Christ stating: Who gave himself for us, that he might redeem us from all iniquity, and purify unto himself a peculiar people, zealous of good works. The problem is many people are selfish and worldly which includes Christians. We have to strengthen ourselves spiritually and live what the bible says and not follow our flesh. We have to learn to stand up for Christ and be zealous to do the work of Christ. However, when we do good works it should be with the right heart and not to receive glory from people.

The bible warns us about doing things to receive glory from men. Matthew 6:16 states: Moreover, when ye fast, be not, as the hypocrites, of a sad countenance: for they disfigure their faces, that they may appear unto men to fast. Verily I say unto you, they have their

reward. Many people including myself at one time try to impress people. God told us in Matthew 6:16 that we will not get a reward from him because we were seeking to impress men. Matthew 6:17 states: But thou, when thou fastest, anoint thine head, and wash thy face. We should take the time to make sure we are not doing things to impress men. Matthew 6:18 states That thou appear not unto men to fast, but unto thy Father which is in secret: and thy Father, which seeth in secret, shall reward thee openly. Therefore, the good we do in secret God will bless us so all can see our blessings.

Many Christians including myself have tried to keep our sins and wrong doings secret. Many of us had paraded our Christianity in hypocrisy and missed out on the true spiritual blessings. Most people think of blessings as money, jobs, material things, and good health. Many Christians live a life of continual struggle because their conversion and dedication to God is not

complete. We have to accept that in our flesh blessings or cursing may seem unfair. Matthew 5:45 states: That ye may be the children of your Father which is in heaven: for He maketh his sun to rise on the evil and on the good, and sendeth rain on the just and on the unjust. God rains on the just and unjust meaning that we will all have trials and tribulation. Our worldly eyes see non-Christians prospering in this world with material wealth and we become envious and desirous of what they have. However, in our spiritual immaturity we don't see what they have is only temporal and worldly while salvation and peace is eternal.

Whether we see it or not there is a movement to discredit the bible and eliminate Christianity. It is time to dig deep and strengthen our spiritual walk through, prayer, fasting, being kind, giving alms, and studying the word of God. Second Timothy 2:15 states: Study to

shew thyself approved unto God, a workman that needeth not to be ashamed, rightly dividing the word of truth. The next verse 2 Timothy 2:16 states: All scripture is given by inspiration of God, and is profitable for doctrine, for reproof, for correction, for instruction in righteousness: Therefore, we must do the word of God not just hear it.

Many people compromise the word of God because they allow things in their life that they know conflict with the word of God. Let's be honest sin is fun because it feels good to the flesh. James 1:22 states: But be ye doers of the word, and not hearers only, deceiving your own selves. The bible says that we deceive ourselves when we allow or participate in ungodly things. One of the largest deceptions right now consists of how we are all going to heaven. The truth is we all can be saved and go to heaven. The reality is all of us will not go to heaven. Matthew 7:14 tells us: Because

strait is the gate, and narrow is the way, which leadeth unto life, and few there be that find it. These words were written in red meaning that Jesus was quoted saying that few will find it referring to heaven. That statement is scary to me because I do not care what men may interpret this to mean I know what I read that Jesus said. However, that does not mean we can't make a mistake or be forgiven for a poor choice because God is full of mercy and He does not want any of us to perish.

Many people like to make things that Jesus says as symbolic or a parable. Yes, Jesus did tell stories in parables but if you really listen there are some eternal truths. In Matthew chapter 5:28 Jesus talks about if a man looks upon a woman lustfully that he commits adultery with her in his heart. Matthew 5:29 states: And if thy right eye offend thee, pluck it out and cast it from

thee: for it is profitable for thee that one of thy members should perish, and not that thy whole body should be cast into hell. Most people would agree that we should not go around plucking our eyes out because we would all be blind eyeless people. Matthew 5:30 states: And if thy right hand offend thee, cut it off, and cast it from thee: for it is profitable for thee that one of thy members should perish, and not that thy whole body should be cast into hell. I used to be confused we did it say if the right hand should offend thee to cut it off and cast it from thee or you could go to hell if you don't. Surprisingly, one day I finally understood the verses.

Jesus was speaking prophetically, spiritually, and reality even though worldly people would quickly reject what I am about to share. We have a spirit body and a human body. The spirit body is the real us but many of us think our physical body earth suit is the real us.

In Matthew 5:28 we lust after a woman in our heart (spirit) not physically. We need to train ourselves not to look with our eyes to lust. We can't help what we see with our physical eyes but we can pluck out our spiritual eyes to not engage in looking lustfully. I believe the reason that we must cut off our spiritual hand is so we won't engage in masturbation. When we lust we can selfishly stimulate our flesh by looking with our eyes and gratifying ourselves with our hand. That is why only the eyes and the hand were mentioned. It works the same way for a woman. If we become taken over by lust when we die our human body will be buried in the earth but our spiritual body will be cast in hell. Henceforth, this is what Jesus said about being cast into hell.

Let's examine a couple of other instances when men were thinking, physically body but Jesus was speaking about the spiritual body. John 3:3 reveals: Jesus answered and said unto him, "Verily, verily, I say unto thee, except a man be born again, he cannot see the kingdom of God." Nicodemus thought Jesus was talking about a man returning to his mother's womb. Christians readily accept that Jesus spoke spiritually.

Matthew 26:61 states: And said, "This fellow said, I am able to destroy the temple of God, and to build it in three days." Men thought Jesus was talking about destroying a building that took 40 years to build and rebuild it in 3 days. Christians readily accept that Jesus was speaking spiritually about his body dying and rising again in three days. Therefore, in my humble opinion we need to be spirit filled and prayed up to receive the word of God and act upon what we are instructed to do.

Physical lust is the greatest compromise in the church. The church has adulterers, fornicators, active

homosexuals, drunkards, drug addicts, pedophiles, and people addicted to pornography just like the world does. Over the past few decades the dress in the church has gotten sexy with low cut tops, high rising skirts and dresses, as well as tight fitting clothes. In some churches you can go to church and lust over the women instead of hearing the message. Church is a place for those who need healing and nothing a person has done should prevent someone from getting to know the Lord. The saying "Come as ye are" has some merit. However, the saying is not "stay as ye are". When we come to receive the word of God we should be coming to find grace and make the changes we need to make to walk with God. Therefore, I am saying that churches should not compromise the standards of God to have higher church attendance.

The truth is the members of the church are on

trial by the world each day. The best way to lead a person to Christ is by your example in your daily walk. By doing the word of God you will not participate in everything the world participates in because if you do you send the message to a non-believer that why do I need to get up early on Sunday/Saturday Sabbath because you are doing the same things of the world? Therefore, those of us who call ourselves Christians can still have fun in this world as long as we are not of the world and are not sinning against the standards that God set.

Chapter 9: Human Beings and Forgiveness

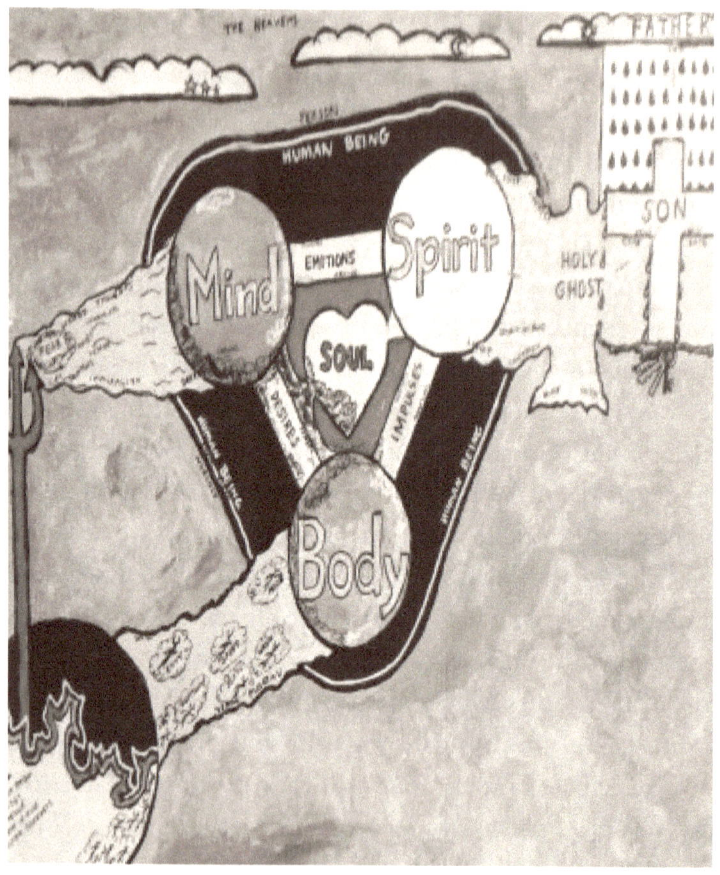

Mind, Body, and Spirit
by The Minister Artist

People who can separate the person from the behavior and hate the sin but not the sinner have an easier time with forgiveness. Before I expound on the topic of forgiveness I want to address the makeup of every human being. Every human being has a mind, body, and spirit. In our human form the mind is the brain. We also have a physical body and a spiritual body. We have a human heart and we have an eternal soul. If our human brain is severely damaged, we will die. If our physical body loses too much blood we will die, and if our heart stops working we will die. However, our mind unlike the brain is eternal. Our spiritual body unlike the physical body is eternal. Our soul unlike the heart is eternal. Insomuch, during our time on earth our physical body houses the spirit of God through the Holy Spirit and Christ to dwell inside of us.

I have heard it said that our soul is our mind, will,

and emotion. Please reference the painting on the previous page titled "Mind, Body, and Spirit". Our will is our desires the things either our body or mind wants. Satan sends messengers to the body to attempt to make a person lustful, gluttonous, or slothful. Lust is the strongest evil force because it not only causes spiritual damage against the person but often involves another person or people and damages their soul. Some people's mind receives satanic implementations of pride, greed, envy/jealousy, and wrath/anger. Pride is probably the worst one because when pride is challenged it can lead to envy, greed, and especially anger. Some people's mind is full of pride which can be negative if a person has pride because the arrogantly think they are above someone by their intelligence, status, finances, looks, physicality, or anything a person

could be prideful about. However, there is a pride that

is often overlooked that must cause God pain. People could cause God pain that will not repent or ask for God for help. God loves us so much more than we understand but the evil one blinds us or consumes us with guilt to the point we condemn ourselves. When we condemn ourselves we are saying that we are not worthy of God's love and we let our past distract our present while dimming the future. Henceforth, desires are collaborations between the mind and the body often without consultation from the spirit.

Emotions are also a strong motivator of human beings. Emotions take place between the mind and the spirit. Most people make the poorest decisions or exhibit their poorest behavior when they are over emotional. When a person is extremely angry they may passively seek revenge or aggressively be violent. When a person is very sad they may passively do self-

destructive things or aggressively seek to take their own

life. Since our mind responds to our flesh through our senses of seeing, hearing, smelling, touching, and tasting our mind competes with our spirit. The carnal mind is like the devil side and our spirit is like the angel side. There is a battle going on inside of us between good and evil. However, when we have strengthened our spirits we develop the emotion of compassion and empathy.

We can strengthen our spirits through, prayer, fasting, reading the scriptures, attending a bible based church, attend bible studies, volunteer to help people in need, spend quality time with your family, and be charitable. We have to be disciplined I the Word of God and not participate in things or activities that the Lord would deem sinful. We have to be disciplined to

enjoy the world but not be of the world. God does want us to be happy he just wants us to put him first,

He wants to bless us but we sometimes become too worldly to hear him. When we only focus on our will or desires we become selfish, stingy, and unwilling to sacrifice our time and money to benefit others. That is where Satan wants us. Satan does not care if we serve him directly and consciously as long as we don't obey the will of God. Insomuch, Satan tries to make his vices look better than the promises of God and make our Lord look undesirable to steal our soul.

Our soul is not our spirit but it is inside of our spirit body which is also inside of our human body. Our soul is really what we love and think about and place value

you on. A person who values God and going to heaven will place value and work at learning the word and doing right by people to please our Heavenly Father.

People who value what the bible says are heaven bound and have treasure in heaven waiting for them. People who are obsessed with fame may work hard to get there

but some people may choose to short cut and make a deal with the devil's people and do something vile to achieve their goal therefore selling their soul to obtain worldly success. A person who is addicted makes what they are addicted to their god. A person could be addicted and still believe they love God but in reality serve their addiction and not serve God. However, God has enough grace for His children to overcome any addiction of the flesh.

Addiction is one of Satan's greatest weapons. The goal consists of getting individual's mind and body to collaborate with each other and ignore the spirit inside of each of us. We are bombarded with words and images corrupting our minds. If we are undisciplined we will entertain the things we hear and see and those things become a temptation to us. The mind and body are the flesh and they often collaborate with one

another to fulfill some form of selfishness. Joyce Meyer wrote a book titled "The Battlefield of the Mind" which sold millions of copies. There truly is a battle over the mind between the unselfishness of the Spirit of God that is within us and our physical body (earth suit) which Satan and his demons continually tempt us unto selfishness. When the mind and body connects without the influence of the spirit the flesh is seeking its desires and wants. Essentially, when a person is carnally minded their mind is controlled by the desires of the body (flesh).

When people give the body too much control over their flesh they make poor choices in pursuit if instant gratification. All people have to feed their body food and give it water to drink. The key to being successful is to eat and drink in moderation. However, when we are not temperate we tend to be excessive. Many Americans over indulge on food and alcohol during the

holidays but people like me do not need a holiday to over indulge. I learned to be temperate during the Corona Virus Pandemic. I no longer had an excuse to be gluttonous, greedy, or addicted because every day seemed the same by focusing on staying safe, healthy, and sanitized. Through the grace of God, I was finally

able to overcome my caffeine addiction. Through grace I overcame the desire for alcohol years earlier because it was hazardous for my marriage. My wife did not play that mainly because of her childhood experience witnessing foolish behavior. The truth was I wanted to overcome my addiction but I did not want my wife to tell me what to do. My carnality which is living to satisfy my flesh can take over when my emotions are high. The bible refers to the mind and body (flesh) as being carnal. However, we do not emphasize the importance of the spirit guiding our lives.

When the mind and spirit connects without the influence of the body we are emotional and often battle thoughts of good and evil. When the spirit connects with the body without influence of the mind (which is not often) it is an impulse. The impulse could be a reaction like rescuing someone in a dangerous situation like saving a person from being hit by a car when you really don't have time to think. It could consist of giving something to someone without thinking about it. You might say that a person is moved by the spirit. Henceforth, whether it is the mind or the body we ought to seek to be spirit lead people.

The spirit is never selfish but the flesh (body) is always selfish. The flesh is never satisfied as it may find

temporary satisfaction that is short lived then it must continue to the next desire. The mind can be selfish too. People with large egos are continually seeking to

make themselves feel superior whether it is their

intelligence, physical appearance, skill level, finances, material possession, or accomplishments. Human Beings need balance between their mind, body, and spirit. When we are too far focused on our minds or our bodies we often make ourselves a god to ourselves and live to serve ourselves. We serve ourselves and fulfill the desires of our flesh therefore we are selFLESH. In simple terms Satan is the master of selfish acts through the flesh and God is the master of unselfish acts through the flesh. Henceforth, in my humble opinion one of the greatest problems in the world is selFLESHness that needs to be overcome. If you really think about it selFLESHness is connected to every sin, disagreement, war, or anything contrary to the will of God. Insomuch, the last book in the bible the Book of Revelations in the KJV Bible refers to

overcoming several times and receiving a reward.

Hopefully, if you understand the origins of selFLESHness you may pray to receive the grace of God through Jesus Christ to overcome your personal areas of selFLESHness.